Sharecropper to Entrepreneur to Pastor

Looking Back and Giving Thanks

Rev. Dr. John Henry Womack

ARPress

ILLUMINATING IDEAS,
EMPOWERING VOICES

ARPress
45 Dan Road Suite 5
Canton MA 02021
Hotline: 1(888) 821-0229
Fax: 1(508) 545-7580

Ordering Information:
Quantity sales. Special discounts are available on quantity purchases by corporations, associations, and others. For details, contact the publisher at the address above.

Printed in the United States of America.

ISBN-13:   Paperback   979-8-89330-457-2
                eBook   979-8-89330-458-9

Library of Congress Control Number: 2024901194

Dedication and Acknowledgements

This book is in honor of my parents, George and Elnora Womack, as well as my wife Bertha whom I love dearly and who has been my greatest friend and supporter for over fifty-eight years. I also dedicate this book to our children, Tonya, John Jr, and Monica, to our grandson, Malik, to my siblings, and to my lifelong mentor, Mr. M.C. Harding. The journey of learning is never achieved solo, and therefore I would like to thank my pastors, theology professors, preachers, teachers, and educators who have shaped my thinking and my life. I would also like to thank my high school classmates and friends for their support during my difficult time in high school.

I have been blessed with a number of friends and business colleagues, who assisted and directed me in the business industry: your help was greatly appreciated. Thanks also go to all of the business employees, and especially to those who served in a managerial capacity so that we could reach a successful goal. I also owe many thanks to all of you who encouraged me and told me not to give up.

Finally, I would like to thank our lifelong friends, Albert and Shirley Hayes, for providing the back cover photograph. This photograph was taken of tobacco fields in Lunenburg County, Virginia in 2015, showing that this part of Virginia is still tobacco country.

Contents

Foreword

In this personal testimony, Pastor Womack has made a valuable contribution to the Christian ministry with the presentation of his life journey. He demonstrates how the hand of God cares for and leads, even in the direst situations.

As John's former pastor, I am pleased that he is sharing this personal testimony of his triumph over adversity. In this compelling story one can witness the struggle of life in its most difficult and challenging reality.

One can be encouraged by this man's significant victory over the many pitfalls of oppressive societal shortfalls. Reverend Womack and his wife, Bertha, demonstrate the power of marriage and family by confident living for Christ against all odds and by working together.

In this book one gets to experience the harsh reality of the exploitative nature of daily life challenges. As a result of reading this text you will seek and find comfort in the Lord.

Rev. Dr. Larry Edmunds
Senior Pastor, St. John's Baptist Church, Woburn, MA (Retired)

Preface

A Salute to Sanctified Tenacity

The Rev. Dr. John Womack's testimony is heart-wrenching and uplifting at the same time. One can't help but ache with him as he shares personal memories of the hardest of labors while young, wrestling to acquire a formal education, striving to be a successful businessman, and toiling in the surprisingly often thankless field of pastoral ministry. Yet, inspired by a faith that grows stronger under fire, Dr. Womack survives and thrives to share a testimony that will bless many who read and hear it.

His testimony is vital for several reasons. First, his is a unique human narrative of what it meant and means to be an African-American male in a country dead-set on deadening his spirit. We have numerous such stories from African-American women offering potent lessons learned through struggle. At a time when young black males are falling again and again due to violence of law enforcement officials, and due to their own self-hatred, we need more testimonies of hope, fortitude, and strength from black men.

Second, Dr. Womack's offerings will add to the dearth of material from African-American pastors. Known for his preaching prowess and leadership powers, the black pastor's personal testimony is still shrouded. We know very little from a black pastoral perspective about what it really means to serve in manifold ways to church and community, while still satisfying the expectations of being a good husband and father. Rev. Womack's willingness to be transparent, and to offer testimony from the shadows and secret places of his heart and soul, will be good nourishment for those serving in pastoral ministry today and tomorrow.

Finally, Dr. Womack is uniquely qualified to offer perspectives from his vantage point as a successful businessman. In partnership with his magnificent, gifted, and devoted wife, Bertha, the Womacks were able to develop thriving businesses at a time when supportive resources were non-existent or in small supply. Yet they were able to successfully climb several entrepreneurial mountains. This book offers invaluable advice on what it takes to succeed in the sacred calling of entrepreneurship.

It is with humble joy and deep gratitude that I present these words of introduction to a book about a life worth living, and a mighty man of God worth listening to. When you are done reading his sincere story, I am sure you will join me in thanking God for and saluting his Sanctified Tenacity.

Kirk Byron Jones, D.Min., Ph.D.
Senior Pastor, Zion Baptist Church, Lynn, Massachusetts
Adjunct Professor, Andover Newton Theological School

Prologue

I met John Womack thirty years ago in the most prosaic and expected places: at church! He was a deacon and a trustee at St. John's Baptist Church in Woburn, Massachusetts, while I was fulfilling my residency requirements for a doctoral degree in social ethics at Boston University and working as an instructor at Curry College in Milton. I'm not quite sure what drew him to me—other than that I had just turned thirty, was already an ordained minister, and was trying to determine a worship home. I am much more certain what captivated me about him.

He stood over six feet tall, was of sturdy build, impeccably dressed, and possessed an unassuming poise that could hardly be overlooked. Although St. John's is a sacred institution, it is comprised of human beings like any other organization. That is to say, it has its flaws and is as much a gossip and rumor mill as presumably most places where people gather. Needless to say, I had heard positive and negative comments about John, but I always followed the rule that I should determine a person's character through direct contact and interaction—not via petty jealousies, insults, and misperceptions folks try to inculcate. Hence, though his reputation preceded my actual tête-à-tête with him, I was instantly enamored of his sincerity, genuine interest in me, and utmost humility. In a way, he acted as if we had been bosom buddies for umpteen years!

As I learned the details of his life from him, I was overwhelmingly impressed. Despite his almost quiescent modesty, if you will, his life story spoke volumes to me and to anyone else who took the time to listen. It was awe-inspiring, encouraging, exhilarating, and downright miraculous! And what was most astounding, it was all for real!

Born into a poor sharecropping family in Virginia, John was determined to better not only his own circumstances, but also the poverty of his relatives. As a youth, he didn't exactly know how he was going to do so, but he maintained his burgeoning faith in the Almighty God and trusted that something good was in store. Hence, early on, he did not have a blueprint of success or a master plan on how to change his status from penury to prosperity. The goal was not to acquire wealth for its own sake; rather, it was to reach a state of affairs where he could have more control over his life and ameliorate the quality of others' lives.

After a stint in the Navy, a fleeting moment back to sharecropping, and time doing factory work, John's opportunity came while he was working for a cleaning company. His work ethic was strong and his understanding of the business deepened. Eventually, it occurred to him that he could be more efficient and productive doing his job as well as more successful in securing contracts for services. Consequently, he set out on his own: first doing work on the side, and then starting his own business: JJS Services, Inc. Within a decade, he had turned a fledgling one–man operation into a sizable, multimillion-dollar corporation!

Most people would consider themselves having "arrived" after their first attainment of wealth. Not John! Commercial success notwithstanding, he believed there was more to life than having money and purchasing power. He had always felt the beckoning of more deliberate service to God that went beyond charitable giving. Knowing he was being led into administering to others, he began to focus on training in religious education and leadership. To that end, he matriculated at Gordon-Conwell Theological Seminary and its urban ministerial academic program. He earned a master's degree in theological studies and a doctor of divinity degree from that institution. After being an associate pastor at St. John's, he branched out into the pastorate at his own assignment, Metropolitan Baptist Church, in Dorchester, where he served for seventeen years.

It has been a privilege to reconnect with John over the past couple of years. In the beginning of the decade of the 1990s, I moved from the greater Boston area to the Midwest. There was a period of time when simply by happenstance we did not communicate that often. However, it was always with fondness that I would reflect upon my association with him: his generosity, upbeat personality, stalwart faith in God, pursuit of becoming more and more like Jesus, creative vision, business acumen, going against the odds, joy over taking risks and being victorious. These are the traits and characteristics of John that nurtured and nourished me on my continual spiritual journey.

In 2014, as director for multicultural education at the University of Northern Iowa, I had the opportunity and the pleasure to invite John to campus to encourage high-school and college students as well as a diversity of community members to take responsibility for their lives and to pursue their dreams and aspirations—ever grounded in their religious faith and philosophical worldview. It was amazing how folks gravitated to him—for he is the genuine article and has practiced what he preaches and teaches. His soft-spoken, methodical speech, his financial advice and expertise, and his Christian witness are infectious, and qualities that any individual could emulate. I am so happy that he is now sharing his story with the world!

Rev. Michael D. Blackwell, Ph.D.
October 30, 2015

Introduction

I write this book with the intention of helping to fulfill my call to the ministry of redemption and the sharing of Christ Jesus. I believe that the call to the ministry is to share the love of Christ. As we receive God's love in whatever forms He chooses, we are expected to share it with others, that they might be converted, inspired, and know that God loves them as well.

Given my background, I hope that readers will see that life's success is partly about academics, but mostly about your perspective of who God is. It is my prayer that my story may help you to understand that God has something for all of us to do, and that we can be equally successful in our individual callings if we have faith in Him. It is my prayer that by exposing a great part of my life will help to encourage you when you feel left out to know that you too can lift up your head, and be all that you desire to be. Another purpose in my writing is to help one to understand that where one come from, the color of your skin, or the lack of an academic degree do not matter: God still has great things in store for all of us. As we know, the God whom we serve is color blind, impartial, "but with God there is no respect of persons." Romans 2:11 (KJV).

I hope that those who read this book will be able to see how God works in good times, bad times, sad times, in times of not knowing, times when you are weak, and in times when you think you are strong. It is my hope that you will be able to see and understand that no matter what life brings, we should always give thanks to God.

Finally, I would like to point out an important feature of the book. This autobiography is structured along thematic lines. While it follows a general chronological sequence, beginning with my childhood and ending with my retirement years, there are sections where it is important to address certain themes more fully even though it involves "jumping ahead" and other places where a brief mention of a future event is made even though that subject is dealt with more completely in a later chapter.

CHAPTER 1

In the Beginning

In the early 1930s God, in his infinite wisdom, provided a way for two great people to meet and to be united in holy matrimony. My father was George Montgomery Womack: as children we called him daddy. Daddy was born in October 1910 in Pittsylvania County, Virginia. My mother was Elnora Goldeburg: as children we called her ma. Mom was born in June 1919 in Lunenburg County, Virginia. Our father had three brothers, one sister, and two half-sisters. In 1926 my father, his siblings, and my grandfather moved from Danville in Pittsylvania County to Lunenburg County. This move involved traveling a total of fifty-eight miles on a horse and a wagon. The Womack family were sharecroppers in Pittsylvania County and continued that occupation when they moved to Lunenburg. While he was growing up our father, in addition to working on a farm with his father, did a lot of day labor earning twenty-five cents per day. He was impressed with his wages because he knew many others who were only earning fifteen cents per day. In reality, dad was paid more because of his skills and success. However, his maximum earnings still totaled only eighty dollars per year for all his hard work. Being the industrious man that he was, dad hired himself out to work from time to time in warehouses and sawmills in the area. He would also cut bushes for the state in order to earn more funds.

Our mother had two brothers and five half-sisters who were also sharecroppers in Lunenburg County. As a child, in addition to sharecropping, our mother worked for twenty-five cents per day plus a meal doing laundry and housecleaning to supplement the family's income.

Mom and daddy got married in 1936 when mom was only sixteen. My parents and their parents were strong believers in God and attended church regularly; the box party where my parents met was a church event. My parents worked the farms of Haney Turrell and Mr. Hervey Powell in Lunenburg County. They also worked as sharecroppers on the farm of Tom and Charlie Garrett: two brothers who happened to be African Americans. Tom and Charlie Garrett were well known and respected in Lunenburg County. They probably owned more land in the county than any other African American. The brothers were very close and they attended our church, which was Flat Rock Baptist Church. They were both trustees of the church and were responsible for overseeing its physical well-being. My parents eventually moved from the Garrett farm because our family was growing and there was a need for a larger home and more acres of tobacco for income.

In 1937, my parents started raising their family. My mother was often sick, but she had enough energy by the grace of God to bear eleven children and to raise ten of them. The second child died as a baby. The firstborn was named Ecynthia, then Geneva (the baby who died) and after her was Alphonso. After having the third child, my mother became seriously ill with tuberculosis. The doctors gave her only a few months to live. My father took the children to his sister's home so that they could be cared for during the time of my mother's illness. The children stayed with my aunt for one year while my mother was in the sanatorium. However, my aunt sent my siblings back home when, to her amazement, she heard that my mother was expecting another child. She figured that my mother must be well enough to take care of her kids if she and my father were increasing the family's roster. During the time of her illness my brother George was born: the first one to be born in a hospital during the time my mother was healing.

At this point in the lives of my mother and family a miracle took place. Mom was stricken with TB in the early 1940s when there was very little medicine or cure for it. There was even less for a family that lived in poverty and who were sharecroppers. My parents could not afford the little treatment that was available, so mom was placed in a sanatorium. At this point mom was only twenty years old but had strong faith and people were praying with her and for her. Through her faith and the prayers of others, healing took place in her body. After the healing her faith grew stronger and stronger, and she became a diligent and lifelong servant of God who worked tirelessly to carry out His will for her life. Mom always visited the sick in her community: she would sit with others who were sick all night long trying to help. She was a devoted missionary for Jesus Christ.

After mom's healing my parents continued to increase the family and mom gave birth to seven more children. Although it looked as if she would live a short life, "Jesus Made Up the Shortage in Her Life."[1] I am the second child after her sickness and number six of the eleven children. In 1942 Daniel was born and then John Henry—"*The steel driving man.*"[2] That is what I was called. We were followed by Allie, Jeanette, Sherman, Jerry, and then Gregory who was the last child and the second to be born in a hospital. All but two of us were born at home. I had the distinction of being the only one born at home that the midwife could not handle by herself. The midwife had to send my father to get the doctor that night. I guess that was a foretaste of my future. It seemed that I came into the world bringing people together to work. My mother says that I was the largest of her children. At birth I weighed in at a little over ten pounds. I started there and grew larger and taller very quickly.

Before I get too far ahead of myself, let me explain how I got from the rolling hills of Virginia Piedmont to the rolling hills of suburban Boston. I was born on July 8, 1944—the son of sharecroppers and the grandson of sharecroppers. I also was destined to become a sharecropper when I grew up. After all, that was all we knew. Interestingly, my walk did not go in that direction. In my adult life, I became a sailor, barber, traveling salesman, custodian, manager of a gas station, an iron worker, fireman, an entrepreneur, and, most importantly, a pastor—but never a sharecropper. At this point in my life, I have concluded that either I have not yet grown up, or have been too busy doing other things and just have not gotten around to becoming a farmer. In fact, I was determined not to become one. Given my strong desire to own something, I suppose sharecropping was not on my list of priorities. Besides that, I am allergic to the hay, tobacco, and other dust that are around a farm.

1. "Jesus Made Up the Shortage" is taken from a sermon I preached based on Matt 6:30–44. In this passage Jesus fed 5,000 people with two fish and five loaves of bread with plenty left over.

2. Around the time of my birth there was a famous song based on an African-American folk hero and legend called "John Henry the Steel Driving Man" about a man driving a steel drill into rock for the placement of explosives in constructing a railroad.

My mother said that the most difficult thing about raising ten children was their schooling, especially since the family moved frequently. I believe it was hard for my mother because she had so many children in different grades and some were beyond her level of education; she felt badly because she was unable to help as much as she would have liked. However, when we moved to the Henry Osborne farm in Blackstone, Virginia the entire family was happy. Although we still had outside toilets, this was the first time that we lived in a house that had electricity and water that came through to the kitchen. The house was back in the woods three quarters of a mile from the dirt road, and three and a half miles from the school. When we moved to Blackstone my grandfather moved in with us. His name was Alexander Womack and at that point he was ninety years old. He passed away three years later. He was the only one of my grandparents whom I knew. We worked on the farm in Blackstone for two years.

When the owner of the farm on which we worked died, his son assumed ownership. One day he told my father that whatever work was not finished on Saturday would be finished on Sunday—the Lord's Day. So my father quit that farm at the end of the year, and we moved back to the east side of Dinwiddie County. We then started school in the city of Dewitt. During the year we were there, I finished the second grade and started the third grade. However, there was a problem.

Each time we changed school systems mid-year, we had to buy new books because each county used different textbooks. Since my family did not have extra money, we children had no new books most of the time. In the middle of the school year, there was also work. Farming/sharecropping was a higher priority than our formal education because our survival depended upon it. So, I spent my early childhood essentially as a part-time student and most of the time with no books from which to study. My mother did some home teaching to make up for lost times in class. Today, if your children miss a significant number of days in school, they might be held back a grade. However, this was not so with us. In fact, part of our practical education was learning the process of farming for it was expected that we would follow in our parents' footsteps.

My father went to school through the third grade, and my mother finished the seventh. I am sure their attendance was worse than their children's. However, as young children we often stayed home from school to work on our farm or on another farm to help them out— and we did not get paid when we did so. It was expected that we would help our parents to succeed in bringing in the produce. In addition, as soon as we were able to work we had to work. I started to work at the age of four and a half, and the same was true for my siblings. At the age of six I learned to drive a tractor in a corn field as we were picking up corn. At first, I thought the tractor drove itself. I did not know that I had to steer it. Fortunately, I did not hurt anybody! In sharecropping, the farm owners looked for large families to work their farms. It was not unusual for several families to work a farm together if the farm was large enough. Wherever we went to work, my father was the foreman. We sometimes would have "cutting parties" and "cutting days" when three or four families would come together to cut wood for heating our homes and for curing tobacco for the whole year. We also harvested together. We worked the farm from Monday to Friday; on Saturdays we sometimes hired ourselves out to earn extra money. Our chief crops were tobacco, corn, wheat, and peanuts. We raised and cultivated our own food in the garden. In Dinwiddie County, we had a large amount of peanuts. This entailed a lot of work: cultivating, weed chopping, and grassing. Because peanut rows were close together, we sometimes had to pull up the grass by hand instead of using a hoe. Harvesting took a lot of time as well. We had to stack peanuts for a six–week drying time. The only good thing about being a peanut farmer was that if the sales after the harvest were not good you could eat some of the nuts. I once ate so many peanuts and pecans that I was sick for three days with very serious stomach pain.

We only lived on this farm in Dinwiddie for one year and then we moved back to our home county, which was Lunenburg. When we moved back to Lunenburg County, we worked the entire two hundred-acre Brickland Farm owned by Mr. Frank Hayden. The owner's house was used by soldiers during the Civil War. Between two families we raised, cultivated, and harvested between twenty and twenty-five acres of tobacco, forty acres of corn, and the other family raised cotton. Each family raised its own livestock. We had hogs, one cow, and lots of chickens. As a family, we would slaughter about ten hogs each year to eat. This was our primary source of meat. Chicken was our second source of meat because there were anywhere from fifty to one hundred chickens around at all times. This also provided our breakfast food such as eggs, fat back from the hogs, and then fried chicken for lunch or dinner. On the farm we also had a lot of squirrel, rabbit, and groundhog meat. We had one cow that produced our milk, but we did not have cows for meat.

Life was hard as sharecroppers, but there was also a sense of freedom and independence. Even though our work time clock began at sunrise and most often ended past sunset, our only earthly master was seasonal change. We may not have had money, but we always had a roof over our heads and food in our stomachs. As sharecroppers, the owner of the farm always provided our housing. We were able to grow our own food and make some of our own clothes: I remember that my first suit was made by my mother. This lifestyle had its freedom, but it also required great discipline. If certain things were not done at the proper time there was a possibility of the harvest not being fruitful. In the 1940s and 1950s, we had to look for neutral ground each year in which to plant the seeds for the tobacco so that the crops would not be diseased. We had to clear the ground—usually by fire and clearing many trees and roots—annually. It was not until the mid-1950s when we could spray the soil and rotate the seeding for the crops and did not have to clear new ground.

The clearing process took place in January or February and we planted the tobacco seeds. We planted wheat and corn in March and April. Wheat and corn for eating were harvested in July and August. Whatever corn had not been harvested in the summer was harvested in the winter during the warmer days. This corn was used as feed for the livestock or for grinding into corn meal. There were also many days in the winter when we could not go to school. We had to stay home and help to pick the corn during that season.

Unlike today's simpler system that allows farm owners to have a larger profit margin, tobacco farming was a time-consuming, labor intensive process with hard-won earnings. We picked two or three leaves at a time and put them on a stick. We then put them in a barn to be cured and that would take four to seven days. After this period of time, the leaves were taken out of the barn, put into a storage house, and there they would stay until we completed the harvesting of all tobacco. At the end of this process, we sorted the leaves by grade and wrapped them for marketing. We stacked the leaves in stalls, restacked them, packed and repacked them to be ready for display at auction and then sold. We had to get up at five o'clock in the morning to work before going to school, and we would start working again as soon as the school day ended. We took a break to eat supper or dinner, then continued working until ten or eleven o'clock at night—sometimes as late as midnight. There was very little time for study. If we did not get it done at study hall in school, it did not get done. Those who grew up on the farm as sharecroppers were programmed to fail if you counted success the way that most people did. There was little opportunity for consistent formal education. During my childhood, there was little opportunity to see or to experience anything beyond rural life and its ritual.

The major drawback was that after working hard all year, there was very little to show for your achievement. No education and no money often spelled doom for the hopes of families in our society—both then and now. Under the 'Jim Crow'[3] segregation of my youth, there was no equal opportunity for me to get ahead, but rather an unequal lack of opportunity. Both black and white children living in rural America in the 1940s, 50s, and 60s lacked options concerning what they could do when they became adults. There were two clear paths. First, we could become what we knew about, and secondly, we could escape from home. If you were black, the odds of escaping the environment were slim. The educational system, supposedly separate but equal, was not equal and did not really prepare anyone for college. Even if you received a good secondary school education, there was often no money available to send you on for a higher education.

Families did not earn enough to save anything. If there exists a disparity between the education of blacks and whites in America today, imagine what it was like for black children in this country in the time of segregation and unequal opportunity. For example, if you were white and your family owned land, you could become a farmer and make money from the people who worked the land for you. If your family had enough money, you might go on to college. In 1964, one year after I graduated from high school, only one in four blacks over the age of twenty-five had graduated from high school. By 2014 that number had risen to 85 percent. In 1964 only 4 percent of blacks obtained a college degree. By 2014 this had risen to only 21 percent, as compared with 34 percent for whites.[4] The chances were that if you were among the few who went to college in rural Virginia—whether you were black or white—you did not return home. There was nothing to do back home except to work the land. Statistics tell us that education is the key to success in this life. Fortunately for me, when formal education was denied, there were other ways of learning.

3. Jim Crow laws were state and local laws enforcing racial segregation in the Southern United States. Enacted after the Reconstruction period, these laws continued in force until 1965.

4. Wolf, "Equality still elusive 50 years after Civil Rights Act."

My time in Dinwiddie was difficult for me as a child. I was often sick and because of that I missed many days from school. I suffered from hay fever, from asthma, and had many colds and other illnesses. I was very shy and kept to myself a lot; I did not make friends easily. We had no books for school because, as I have already mentioned, we sometimes moved in the middle of a school year to another county where the books were not the same. We had just purchased books and there was no money to purchase any more. Due to all of these factors I felt left out, sad, and left behind. Wherever we moved, we attended church and Sunday school. Lunenburg County was "home," and Flat Rock Baptist was my home church. The service was once a month on first Sunday. We went there every first Sunday, but it was often not possible for the entire family to go because some of us did not have clothes or shoes to wear. It was also hard for the entire family to fit into one car so we took turns. When you had to stay home it was a long and lonely day. I recall some lyrics that stick with me even today, although I do not know the origin or author of the song: "That Mother's Child, Sure See's It Hard When Your Mother Is Gone." I remember those days so very well, going from window to window looking to see if the family was home. When we lived in Blackstone, the church was across the road from the school house, which was three and a half miles away from home. In Darvills, which was located in the western part of Dinwiddie County, the church was a mile away. However, in east Dinwiddie County, we had a five-mile walk or ride to church.

It was during one of these walks that I had one of my first encounters with racism. On this day some white boys made my brothers and me very upset. As we walked along the road and it was very hot, a car stopped and the driver asked if we were tired of walking. He stopped up ahead—apparently to pick us up, we thought. We started running to the car expecting a ride. Instead, the boys inside the car yelled out, "If you're tired of walking, then start crawling" and then they pulled off. Sometimes we would be walking the road and white people would ride by and yell, "Get out of the road Nigger." Lord knows that we needed Jesus to help us deal with such madness and to grow up to be the relatively healthy, sane adults we are today. Flat Rock Baptist Church and friends were far away, and we did not stay long enough in Dinwiddie to make new friends. The Lambert family, our first cousins, lived about thirty-five miles away: they were our home away from home. When we attended church at Flat Rock we usually ended up having dinner at the Lambert family's home. They worked along with us on every farm, except in Nottoway County.

When we lived in Nottoway County, we sometimes walked to the drive-in theater and climbed a tree to watch the movies. We were also able to make a little money as kids. The owner of the drive-in asked our father if he could hire us to clean up the yard at the theater. For this we would be paid forty dollars per month to pick up the trash—but the funds went to dad. Our bonus for doing this work was that we would usually find some extra money on the ground because the theater was heavily used by the members of the Armed Forces who came from Camp Pickett in Blackstone, Virginia.

A difficult aspect of my young life was that my father was not around very often on the weekends. Once I was very sick with a cold that turned into pneumonia and my dad was not around to take me to the doctor. Times like these were very difficult and hurtful, and in those days there were no phones to call for help. I also remember that once my two older brothers got up early in the morning to do some work with the tractor before going to school, and my older brother lost half of his finger trying to hook up the equipment. My father was not home very much due to the fact that sharecropping did not provide sufficient income to take care of the large family that he had. To have extra income he became the manufacturer of moonshine. Each week this would keep him from home two or three nights a week. He not only manufactured moonshine but also sold it wholesale and retail. It was my understanding that this was hard work because it took a lot of strength to carry all the equipment and material through the woods at night to a creek of water where the moonshine could be made. My father had others who worked with him, and it took as long as seven to ten days to produce a fully cured production of corn liquor to sell.

In addition to this, I learned at the age of eleven or twelve that my father was involved in extracurricular activities outside of our home. For this reason dad was not at home on many weekends. This was devastating to me as a young boy and it tore deeply into my heart. I remember how I used to walk the road through the woods of the farm, praying and hoping that nothing had happened to my dad. We did not know all that was going on, and we were sorry for our mother because of what she was going through as well. There were three brothers who were older than me, and in many cases the four of us took on the brunt of the work at home and on the farm when dad was absent. There was only one year and a few months difference between our ages. A good amount of this time my oldest sister was living in New York. We often tried to encourage our mother to go and spend some time with her because Ecynthia was her oldest daughter, but mom refused to leave us home alone. These were very difficult times for us as a family, but somehow God made it possible for us to survive through it all. As children you always love your parents, and we loved and respected our father even as we went through these hard times. We had to do so because our mother trained us that way. Mom taught and showed us how to always walk in a godly way.

My older brothers left home carrying a grudge against our dad. During those times, being young, we did not fully understand forgiveness. And, considering all that we went through, it was also hard to forgive. Many of us left home before God placed it in our hearts to forgive our dad. I can remember speaking to my older brothers about this, telling them that we needed to forgive our father and think more about mom and our younger siblings whom we left at home. I believe that as we all got older we understood Satan and his temptation. As we grew older we were also able to understand that no one is perfect. While we disagreed with and hated many of the actions of our father, we found a way through God to forgive him. We were able to better understand that he was a hard worker and that he meant well, but was led astray by Satan's temptation.

One good part about our life on the farm was that we all learned to work. Each of us had chores to do in the morning and in the afternoon that were over and above the regular farm work. There was the cow to milk morning and afternoon, and wood to be prepared for the kitchen stove and for the big heater that was used in the winter to warm the house. There were hogs, dogs, chickens, and horses to be fed in the morning and again in the afternoon. As one child graduated from high school and moved on with his or her life, there was a chore that was left for someone else. As we got older, we would have to train the next person what to do. When I graduated from high school it was very difficult because there were five children younger than I was and the next two were girls. The girls could not perform all of the work that we as boys had been doing. The next oldest boy was only eleven years old when I left home. I was leaving a lot of responsibility for them and it was difficult for mom because she was getting older and her health was failing. One of the things that I tried to do was to make sure that I assisted the family that I left behind in every way that I could. From the beginning of my time in the armed service I made out an allotment that went to my mother each month to assist the family at home. I also helped the family in purchasing school clothes and other needed items around Christmas time.

Although I had nothing and was on the verge of knowing nothing, God provided people along the way to encourage me, to give me hope, and to teach me. Among my family, neighbors, teachers, and friends were strong black role models for me to follow. Although they were not perfect people, yet they provided me with a glimpse of the possibilities that lay before me as I walked down the road of life. They taught me the meaning of having faith, courage, and to never give up. They challenged me, loved me, and nurtured me by shaping me into the man that I am today. I hope that the legacy they placed in me will continue for many generations to come as I share my life, knowledge, and wisdom with others.

The first people who influenced me were my parents. They taught me how to survive in a hostile world and to stand up for what was right. My father even stood up to his white boss—the farm owner who said that we would have to work on Sundays if Saturday's work was not completed—without being afraid of the consequences. There was also a time when the owner of the farm told my father that he wanted the boys not to go to school one day but instead to do some kind of work on the farm. My father told him that his boys were going to school and that it was not the owner's call to tell him when to keep his boys home. Dad taught us to work hard and to do an excellent job. He was always the foreman on any farm where the family worked: he was a leader and a very skilled worker. Dad repaired most of the equipment on the farm at no cost to the owner. My father could take out the engine of his car, overhaul it, and put it back in within a three-day time frame. My mother, in addition to being our home teacher, was also the spiritual leader of the home. She made sure that we went to church and Sunday school every week. She was an example to me of faith in the time of sickness and trouble. I also learned the importance of family through my parents. Because my father was not around as often as he should have been, I was determined to spend time with my family.

I made a vow to the Lord before I left home that if I ever had a wife, I would make sure that she would not have to work. This vow was made because it hurt me to see how hard my mother had to work, even while she was pregnant. Many times she started the day with the morning dew and would be drenched in sweat, handling tobacco and lifting in the fields. I am happy to say that the Lord heard my prayer: after our first child was born my wife did not work. Once our children were in school she went to school to get her degree, worked in her field of study for a few years, and then worked periodically in our family's business.

Uncle Daniel was my father's brother. He was another great role model for me. He walked wherever he wanted to go and did almost anything he wanted to do. In addition to the challenges that faced him being born black in America around the turn of the century, he became blind at the age of nine years. His life was one of faith. As a deacon, he sang for many years in the church. Uncle Daniel was part of a singing group called *The Ideal Spiritual Singers*: he played guitar and my father sometimes sang with them and drove them around. They sang on the radio in Crewe, Virginia every Sunday at nine o'clock in the morning. Uncle Daniel taught me that no handicap can hinder someone who is determined, creative, and who depends on God for guidance and strength. God is the master of obstacles.

We four oldest brothers were comrades. We did everything together. People told me that when we were kids, if you were a friend of the Womack brothers, you did not have to worry about enemies because we were so much larger than everyone else. No one dared bother them or their friends. Like the generation before us, we started a singing group—*The Spiritual Five* better known as *The Womack Brothers*.

My extended family was always important to me. One of the figures that stood out was Aunt Callie King. She was my father's sister and a mother of nine. She worked as a farmer and her family were tobacco sharecroppers as well. She did everything, especially when her husband was in the hospital. I stayed with her from time to time when we lived in Blackstone. Aunt Callie said that I told her my dreams of buying a car, raising cows and hogs, and taking care of my family. She also said that I used to share my imitations of my mother and father conversing together. I must have truly trusted her.

I have great love and affection for each of my sisters and brothers, and admire each of them in their individual ways. There were things that they could do that I could not do, and I always tried to do everything they did even though I was much younger.

When we moved from Nottoway County my oldest sister Ecynthia did not move with us because she had only half a year to go before graduation. My mother and sister were able to talk my father into allowing her to stay with a family that lived close by so that she would be able to finish school in Nottoway County. Upon graduation she attended St. Paul's College in Lawrenceville, Virginia, where she went to school for one year to be a seamstress. She went to New York to work that summer, but never returned to Virginia. Ecynthia was of great help and a jewel to our family. She worked hard in New York and always sent mom a little money whenever she was able, simply because she knew the circumstances in which we lived. She helped the family in any way she could. I recall her sending us our first used television. (Unfortunately, we could never get it to work because we could not afford a TV antenna.) As soon as each of us matured and left home, Ecynthia would make room and allow her sisters or brothers to stay at her home until we were able to find jobs and get our own places to live.

In 1980 my brother Daniel, who was one and a half years older than me, was killed while he was in the Army. He was a staff sergeant and had spent fourteen years serving our country. Unfortunately, he was killed by a person who was also in the Army. The incident involved what today might be called road rage. However, there were several other factors that are important to mention. Before Daniel was shot three times on that day in 1980, he was paralyzed on one side and was so harmless that he had talked about getting out of service on disability. The shooter was Caucasian—and he and Daniel knew each other in service. Daniel was in an interracial marriage to a Caucasian lady. The shooter was set free by the North Carolina courts, which stated that the shooting was on the basis of self-defense. However, this could not have been true because Daniel was not carrying any kind of weapon. The jury was all white with the exception of one black man who was about eighteen years old. In addition to the possibility that the event had racial components, I experienced personal anguish over my brother's death. The weekend that he was killed, I had planned to visit with him. However, I was very tired and made the decision not to drive from Virginia, where I was visiting with my parents, to North Carolina and then back to Boston in time for work on Monday morning. I always wondered whether the incident would have occurred if I had been with him. In many ways Daniel and I did not share the same ideas, even though we were very close. I admired him for his ability to make music, play the guitar, dance, and to just be a fun guy. In his last year in high school, we played football together. He played the right tackle and I was the left tackle. When the coach would call off the line up for the game he would always say tackle Womack and Womack.

Two of my longtime friends from home were Walter "Sonny" Smith and Alvin Ellis. We met in the fourth grade. We attended school, ate lunch, and did farm chores together. When I returned home during the ensuing years, we still found time to see each other. Another friend was James Jackson—whom we called Monkey Jackson. He lived about two miles away and, since we had no television, we would often walk to his home on weekends to watch TV—mostly westerns such as the Roy Rogers Show, and, on Sunday evenings, the Ted Mack show. James's mother was a good person because the television was in her bedroom and she allowed us to watch TV there. James remains a good friend to this day. Companionship also came through sports, and many friends were football players: Robert Hardy had access to his father's car and we would frequently go places together; Louis Watson was a close friend and often described as one of the Womack brothers. Bobby Williams kept me apprised of the young ladies who were interested in me—specifically one in the city of Kenbridge where her father owned a restaurant. There were also many friends who helped me on the farm, making it possible for me to attend football practice.

There were not many black people who owned their own land when I was growing up. Many of the previous generation had lost their farms during the depression, and the white people reclaimed ownership. An exception to this was Mrs. Beatrice Lambert, who was my mother's friend since the second grade. She maintained her land and farmed it. I marveled at her because she could drive a tractor and a truck as well as any man I knew. She was also one of our Sunday school teachers, clerk of the church, and worked in a hospital. Through her example, I learned that African-American people could own something and be successful at their work.

When we moved back to Lunenburg County, we lived in a house with no indoor bathroom and no running water. However, it was big enough to hold all of us. We—the four oldest boys—grew up in a 12 x 12 room that was in the peak of the house with a tin roof. Four teenage boys in one room of that size can be very difficult at times. There were many concerns about who was supposed to clean up, and who was always messing up. We often could not afford mattresses for our beds, so my mother would cut flour bags and sew them together and we would stuff wheat straw into them to sleep on. We walked to Sunday school, which was seven and a half miles away.

Behind every achievement that I made along the way, my 4-H Club leader, Mr. Milton Harding, had a tremendous effect on my life and on the lives of my family. It was Mr. Harding who, when he was secretary of Lodge #214, helped us by connecting my father to the mill for extra work. He taught me not only to be a good farmer, but also a great deal about strategy, hard work, and excelling at whatever I did. He gave me the opportunity to expand my horizons beyond Lunenburg and the surrounding counties through summer 4-H Camp and state competitions. One of my dreams was to team up with Mr. Harding to teach agriculture in Africa. This dream never materialized as we both grew older and Mr. Harding passed away. As a member of the 4-H Club I had projects to do. I raised an acre of sweet potatoes on two occasions, and put everyone else in the family to work, picking and sorting them. Another one of my projects was raising tobacco for a state competition. In that year, the projects were judged without regard to the race of the presenter. Each person's produce was judged on its own merit being identified only by a number. The judges kept asking Mr. Harding who was the presenter of a particular entry, but he would not let them know until after the winner had been decided. I was that winner. My tobacco had triumphed! I do not think the white people liked the idea that someone black could win over their children. That was the last time that the competition was ever held.

My three brothers and I bought our first car in 1956. It was a 1951 Hudson: the cars we owned were handed down as each one of us moved on, and it ended up being owned by Daniel and me. Danny was an aggressive driver. He was like my father, a fast and sometime reckless driver whom no one wanted to meet on the road. He would tear up a car in a few months, and we would have to walk for the balance of the year. We disagreed over his driving habits and other things, and agreed to alternate weekends to use the car. Once, Mr. Harding asked me to take a group of 4-H Club members to Virginia State for a week of camping; Daniel was angry because I had the use of the car for the whole week.

I met my best friend, Bertha, in the eighth grade; her parents, like mine, were sharecroppers. I told people that I was attracted to her because she was very small and short: I thought she needed protection. However *I fell in love with her*. I also gave her credit for making sure that I did not starve. My family did not have enough money for me to buy lunch every day, so Bertha and I made sure that we shared whatever we had with each other. Bertha is a beautiful person inside and out. Although we never officially dated in high school, yet we did things together. This included flunking Mrs. Drummond's English class. I had other friends and Bertha would sometimes get very upset. I felt that she was saying to them, *"you have him now, but in the end he will be mine."* It turned out that she was right and I am happy that it worked out that way.

It was God's plan all along: Bertha is still my best friend even after fifty-eight years of marriage. If it were not for segregation, we may never have met. I passed by the all–white Kenbridge High School in Kenbridge, Virginia to go to Victoria, which was fifteen miles away. There I attended Lunenburg High School. The law mandated that if we had separate schools, they must be equal. Many communities in the South built separate schools for blacks and whites on similar floor plans to fulfill the letter of the law. However, the schools were by no means equal. The black schools lacked the equipment and resources that the white schools possessed. In spite of the mistreatment, we had excellent teachers who did more than make up for other things we were missing.

In high school, there were teachers who pushed me to excel. Besides Mrs. Pauline Drummond, there were Mrs. Annie Holmes and Mr. Galvin Jenkins. The principal of Lunenburg High at that time was Mr. Waddill Craghead. These teachers invested themselves in the students and exposed me to a world of ideas beyond the farm and the county. Mr. Jenkins taught farm mechanics, electricity, woodworking, and agricultural education. He later became the principal of the school. Mr. Jenkins told people that I was an excellent student—but I was not. Rather, I was your typical below-average scholar. I believe that he had confused me with my brother George. George was the excellent student in the family. We always expected him to be a preacher and so we called him that. He was the one who I looked up to in my family. Rather than academics, football was my love. I was the co-captain of the high school football team. My high school days were full of study, work, and walking. We took the bus to school, but I often walked home after 4-H or other activities. My friends and I would sometimes walk several miles to go to the movies.

When I was younger and still living on the farm in Virginia, I spent a lot of time alone. When we worked in the fields I was often ahead of the rest of the family: rather than talking, I did my work and a lot of thinking. When we had free time I would walk along the road, sometimes picking berries. At other times I walked through the woods alone as I went from place to place visiting people. Sometimes I went to my friend Alvin Ellis's house, which was located about four miles away from where I lived. Sometimes I would travel to my friend Monkey Jackson's place. I found myself thinking and planning, hoping and dreaming for the future. This has carried over to my adult life. I find that I listen in order to learn, rather than talking about something I know nothing about. I suppose I was quiet and introspective. I spent a great deal of time seeing things that others did not see. I took time to think and plan. Even now, I like being alone for the same reasons.

Many of my hopes and dreams have come true—yet, I find that I do not focus on accomplishments. Rather, I am constantly trying to find new ideas to focus on in order to move forward in life. God has instilled this in me—recognizing that I am not the most brilliant person in the world nor the most happy-go-lucky, but God has given me the abilities that I have and called me to enhance them in order to help others. I often think that people would be amazed if they knew some of the acts of kindness that I would still like to do in my life—ideas that God has placed in my heart and that may seem impossible to some, but not to God. I believe in giving a person a chance no matter how bad the situation may be because I know that God provided many opportunities for me when it appeared to many that I was a failure.

Friendship is something that is important to me, but it has become elusive with the passage of time. Some of those whom I thought of as friends always seemed to move away from me. Friends are supposed to accept people as they are, and changes in the status of our lives should not change the quality of friendship. My friends may have thought that I did not want a relationship with them as I theoretically moved up the social ladder. However, that was not true. I never changed, and things and positions do not make me change. I still liked doing the old things with old friends. For many years after high school I never saw my football friends Louis Watson, Robert Hardy, and James May 'Boojack.' Of my two navy buddies, I only stay in touch with one. Now that I am a minister, I have fewer friends than ever. My business friends, even the ones who are Christians, do not want to spend time with me unless it is at a social engagement. They are reluctant to fellowship with me at religious gatherings; perhaps they suspect that I have become a "holy roller." Pastors sometimes cannot befriend each other due to competition and conflict. There are several other pastors with whom I spend time, but our relationships are not as intimate as they could be. At this point in my life, I need friends more than ever. Since they are few and far between, I must depend on the Lord to satisfy my needs.

As I come to the end of this chapter, I would like to say a few more words about my parents to complete their story and their important influence on my life. God was able to allow me to forgive my father and, in doing so, also placed it on my heart to do all that I could to assist mom, dad, and our younger siblings. In 1965 Dad was incarcerated after being arrested by the law for manufacturing corn liquor/moonshine. This was during my time in the military. After he did his six months of incarceration he returned home to the farm and was met by a very disgruntled farm owner. My older brother who had returned home had now left again and was serving in the military. This was the year my parents stopped sharecropping and my father was able to obtain a job in a furniture factory. I believe that this was the point in his life when dad made a change and came closer to God.

When I look at these circumstances I can see how God allows a mess to bring out our best. Had this not happened to my father he perhaps would have continued doing what he was doing. One year after I was married I had to stop the allotment that was going to my mother but I continued to work and to help my parents in any way I could. When I got out of the Navy my 4-H club mentor Mr. Harding and I worked hard to pursue obtaining one acre of land to build the first home for my parents. This was accomplished in 1971. The three-bedroom home and land cost fifteen thousand five hundred dollars. The payments were seventy-two dollars per month because of my parents' low income. These payments were later reduced to fifty-three dollars per month. I paid the mortgage off in the late 1980s and our parents lived there happily in their first home. The only new car that my parents ever had was a 1954 Chevrolet. Dad loved that car and he drove it like it was his pride and joy. It was taken away from us in 1955 when dad was arrested for transporting moonshine. In 1985 I gave my father and mother a new Chevy S-10 pickup truck because their vehicle had just about played out. This was their first new vehicle since 1954. After eleven years with the S-10 truck, I gave them a new 1996 full-size Chevy pickup truck, and dad was one happy camper. He gave the S-10 pickup to a gentleman who had been helping him out.

In the mid-90s mom became seriously ill and was not able to do very much. She was mostly bedridden during the last five years of her life. Even during this period mom remained faithful, and her trust and belief in God became stronger than they had ever been. There were times when she would be sitting and you would hear her just say, "thank you Jesus." We would go home to be with mom and to encourage her, but in most cases mom ended up encouraging us. She was a strong lady and I am sure that her faith in God is what made her the person that she was. Mom passed away on April 15, 2004; at the time of her death she and my father had been married for sixty-nine years. Dad became sick and passed away four years later on the same day: April 15, 2008.

The most important influence in my life was and is the influence of God. I grew up in the church. I was eleven or twelve years old when God called me to seriously commit to Him. As a young person, I had many dreams. I dreamed almost every night, although most of the dreams I could not interpret or convey to anyone else. Sometimes it troubled me and I could not sleep because of it. During one of my few leisure times, around the age of eleven or twelve, I was lying in a tobacco field off of Route 138 in Lunenburg County looking at the sky and I fell asleep. It was a somewhat cloudy day; the sun would peak through intermittently. While asleep, I saw God's face in the sun, saying nothing but smiling at me. I saw a vision of God there in the clouds: there was a smile on His face as though He was saying, "I am going to smile on you." I told no one about this dream for almost forty years. Now, as I look back over my life, I can see that God was calling out to me and smiling at me, simply because I looked down on myself during my childhood and felt that I was less than others: a nobody. I looked up to my sisters, brothers, and friends, feeling that I was not good enough to measure up to them. I believe that this feeling was partially rooted in a scene that took place one evening when I was eight or nine years old. Our family was visiting with our aunts and uncles who lived up north in Baltimore, New York, and New Jersey. On this particular night eight or nine of us were in the car. Our aunts evaluated us children as we emerged from the car. As I got out of the car, they said that I did not look too well, and would not amount to much in life.

I knew from that moment when I saw God's face in the sun on that cloudy day that He was real, and that He had plans for my life. My problem was that I could not understand His purposes or what I was to do, and it was not until my adult life that I really said "Yes" to the Lord. At that time, I tried to obey my parents and pay attention to what I learned in Sunday school and in church—but it was not easy. I always wanted to live the way God wanted me to but for some reason I felt incapable of doing so. Satan was very tempting and I did not know what God had in store for me, but I decided that I was going to pay attention. I continued to dream dreams at night and to see visions by day. I waited for the unfolding of His plan and do so even now. God has been and will always be my most constant friend.

CHAPTER 2

Educational Background
and Experience

I turned six years old on July 8, 1950, and began my school life in September of 1950. I was placed in the first grade in West Dinwiddie County School while living in Darville, Virginia. I vividly recall my first day of school and the first time riding a school bus. I was very nervous, but I had three brothers and an older sister riding the same bus. There were some difficult aspects of that first year in school. There were two large brothers in our class who had been in the first grade for a number of years. They had a habit of stealing lunches; on many days, my lunch came up missing along with the lunches of others. Another bad memory about the first grade concerned our teacher, Mrs. Gladys Madison. She was very hard and seemed to dislike dark-skinned people. She would use the yardstick to punish us; when she did so, she would turn the yardstick upside down and hit us on the back of our hands. I also remember that, even at such a young age, I had a crush on a girl name Ada; I may have been the only one who knew she was special to me. However, a fun memory included my friend, Junior King. On most days we would eat lunch together. One particularly memorable day he invited me to have lunch with him and he recalled that I told him, "No man, I have bologna today for lunch." The reason I refused was that I did not want to share. Bologna was a big deal for us during those days. Most of the time we had fat back, or fried white potatoes in a biscuit.

Since my parents were sharecroppers, I only attended that school for half of the first grade due to the fact that my parents would often move at the end of December or the beginning of January—during the middle of the school year. This was because of the farming season. In January of 1951 we moved to Nottaway County. When my dad took us to school, the teacher asked him if this was my first year in school and he responded in the affirmative. Thus, she put me in what they called primary grade, which was a grade just before the first grade, somewhat like nursery school or kindergarten. Consequently, I was detained for one year early on in my school life, which resulted in my graduation from high school at the age of eighteen and not seventeen.

In Nottaway County, we had to walk three miles every day to school because there was no bus running from our area. During the first half of the year, my school day would end at two o'clock in the afternoon, while my brothers' school day would not be over until three o'clock. Hence, I had to walk the full three miles home each day alone and this included three-quarters of a mile back in the woods where our house was located. Sometimes I was very afraid because I heard all kinds of scary sounds in the woods. Each Friday during lunchtime, we usually had a fish fry with corn bread and a talent show. This was when my three brothers and I began our little singing career. The four of us sang as a quartet during the talent show—we sang songs like "Down by the Riverside." Mrs. Edmonds was my teacher and Mrs. Ruffing was the principal of the two-room school, which ranged from primary through the seventh grade. While walking to school, we had to cross a railroad track. Sometimes, the train stopped and blocked our passage. On cold mornings when the train was very long, we would crawl under one of the train cars very fast in order to get to school on time. In retrospect, we realized that our actions were dangerous and inconsiderate.

We lived in Blackstone for two years. Around the beginning of 1953 we moved again. This time we moved to the northeast part of Dinwiddie County. I was in the second half of the second grade and attended DeWitt School. While we lived there, we did not have to walk to school for we were able to take the bus again. My schoolteacher's name was Mrs. Lomack and the school principal was Mr. Bernard Morgan. There were two school buildings: one building housed the first through the third graders, and the other building housed the fourth through the seventh graders. I was at that school for only one year: one-half year in the second grade and one-half year in the third.

At the beginning of 1954, we moved back to Lunenburg County, where I attended Miss Shields's class at the Asbury Elementary School. This was a two-room school whose principal was Mr. Harris. He was also the teacher for grades four through seven, and the next school year I was in the fourth grade. Eventually, he left and Mr. Taylor became the principal. At this point, I went from riding the bus to walking again. However, the walk was just a little less than one mile to school. During my second year the bus began to come past where we lived and I had the choice of riding the bus or walking to school. One of the advantages of going to a two-room school in a small community was the opportunity to associate with teachers not only during class hours but also during school breaks; the teachers usually lived in the neighborhood and went to the local church as well. For example, Miss Shields turned out to be a lifelong friend and teacher. Many of the friends that I made at Asbury did not finish the seventh grade and did not go on to high school because of farm work. Still, a majority of them remained my friends. It was at that school that I was also introduced to the 4-H Club and met my lifelong mentor, Mr. Harding, who was the local farm agent for Lunenburg County.

It has already been made clear that the 4-H Club was a major influence on my life; in fact, it is not too much to say that it was the organization that inspired me the most during my early teenage years. The 4-H Club was a part of our school experience. It was good to see Mr. Harding drive on to campus, because this meant that we would have a break from our normal school activities in order to attend his club meeting for at least one hour. It was during these meetings that I learned a lot about parliamentary procedures, farming techniques, tractor driving techniques, tractor maintenance, and engine repair—how to take them apart and put them back together again. Participation in the club also provided opportunities for us to meet other teenagers outside of our county, such as when we attended the 4-H Club Convention for one week at Virginia State College in Petersburg during the month of July.

In September 1959, I began the eighth grade at Lunenburg High School in Victoria, Virginia. My homeroom teacher that year was Mrs. Annie Sue Holmes, and the principal was Mr. Craighead. Mrs. Holmes was also my civics teacher that year, and because I was behind in class and not able to attend school very much doing the months of September and October, she allowed me to catch up by doing a special project. That project was one that I had started doing in the seventh grade. I designed a map of the

United States utilizing scraps of cut up newspaper put on a large piece of board with starch, and outlining all the states within the map. This project allowed me to get extra credit and to pass the subject for the year.

This period in my life was not only very exciting but fearful. For example, I experienced my first lengthy bus ride to school—fifteen miles—and my first time being around so many other students at once. This campus housed students from kindergarten through the twelfth grade. Many of the students had gone to small elementary schools in different parts of the county and were now coming together at the high school. In addition, this new experience was exciting because I had more than one teacher during the course of a day. Also, it was stimulating to be able to get up and move around after an hour and fifteen minutes of sitting in class. We were able to walk to another class and perhaps meet someone new along the way, or to say "Hello" to a relative who might be an upper classman. Classes that took place in high school covered subjects such as agriculture, welding, wood work, and auto mechanics. The curriculum also included sports activities such as baseball, football, and track—all of which brought me great enthusiasm. When many of these activities started, I naturally wanted to be a part of them. Later, I found out that I could not play any sports until I was in the ninth grade.

My first year in Lunenburg High School was thrilling and perhaps one of the most memorable times that I had encountered. I was growing up very fast and this particular year brought a new chapter into my life. It was in the eighth grade that I met the one whom I would marry. It happened in September, the best month of my life, for I met Bertha in our home room first period. We met at this early age, but the only dating that we were able to do for the next five years was moving from one class to the other. Her mother did not allow her to go out on dates. I suspected Bertha knew that she was saving herself just for me. Needless to say, Bertha was a very strong person and truly committed to me: I say this because I was a little impatient and did not pass up the chance to date other girls. This must have made it very hard for her at times, but her faith in God made it possible for her to wait. I am happy that God also made it possible for me to avoid becoming overly involved with other girls to the point that Bertha and I did not remain as friends. It seemed as though we were predestined to be together for the remainder of our lives. Although at the time I did not know we would be married, I knew that God had placed Bertha in my presence and in my heart for a reason.

In the month of August 1960, a letter went out from the school stating when the first football practice would be held. I was an early arrival on that day, and Mr. George Allen, the coach, had not yet arrived at football practice. I had a strong interest in football—an interest that has stayed with me even to this day. My brother George had just graduated from high school. He had played football, and there was a lot of talk around our home about his games—making me want to play all the more. My oldest brother Alphonse ran track in high school and was very good as well. Prior to the fall of 1959, I had never seen a football game played. In addition to football, I was very interested in baseball. By the end of my first year at Lunenburg, the school did not have the funds to keep the baseball program because all of the equipment for baseball was stolen during the summer. I was only able to play baseball with the outside county teams in our area. Some of the older men organized a team, and we learned to play with them. We would travel from county to county and play other organized teams on makeshift baseball fields.

The 1960 football season went well. I had some difficulty keeping passing grades, and a number of my teachers suggested that I not attend football practices that occurred during class time. I was happy about interrupting our classes to play football. However, doing so did not help our grades and teachers strongly objected to practices during class hours. The reason that practices were held during a class period or two was because most of the students were part of farm families, and we had to work the fields after school. The next year, practice occurred after school and my getting home late became a problem. Sometimes, I would arrive home very late because I did not have a car and the buses were gone by the time practice was over. I often hitchhiked my way home and many days I had to walk. I must say that I had some very good friends in high school. When I got behind on work at home, some of the boys would come home with me and help out on the farm so that I would be able to play in the games on Fridays. These boys lived in town and did not have farm work to do, but they were willing to help my brother and me in this way throughout the four years of my high school football career.

One of my learning experiences when I played football occurred with an older classmate who would regularly beat me pretty badly. He had been on the team for three years playing tackle. He beat me so badly one day that I decided I was not going to allow him to do that to me anymore. From that point on, I became a strong football player. For four years I played left tackle for all forty-eight minutes of each game. I also became the co-captain of the team during the last two years of school.

All of my teachers in high school wanted to see their students do well. I am sure it was heartbreaking for the teachers to see many of their students, whom they knew had the ability to excel, unable to learn and perform well. This predicament occurred because students had numerous school absences resulting from the fact that their labor was needed on the farm. Although going to football practices during the week had adverse effects, I attended almost all of the games because Thursday and Friday were the weekdays when we were finished with the weekly harvests and were able to go to school. However, at the beginning of the school year in September through the end of October, and sometimes most of November, I only went to school for one, two, or three days a week.

These were very difficult times: simultaneously trying to get an education and maintain a livelihood as sharecroppers. Since I had a large family, my siblings and I would rotate school attendance. Sometimes we took turns staying home from school to prepare the tobacco. The children who went to school would be charged with bringing notes and homework assignments back home from the teachers. This took place so that if the others went the next day, they could turn in their homework or at least study it so that they would know what was going on in the classroom. Along with the homework, if my friends saw a sister or brother at school, they would send a little note saying "Hi." If they were in my class, they would tell me what the work would be for the next day.

I do not know how I made it through high school, but by the grace of God I did. My grades were very low; therefore, I showed very little potential for being a candidate for college. However, there is something that people need to understand: there are many things a person can learn while working the fields on a farm, planting the seeds, seeing them grow, and understanding the ground. One can see how God waters the land and provides the needed sunshine at the appropriate times. There are many farming practices that can be applied to other things that people do throughout life. A lot of it is simply common sense—something that students do not always get in a classroom setting.

An exciting thing that happened in the late fall of 1958 as I started high school was that my three older brothers and I were given two acres of tobacco. The sale of the tobacco made it possible for us to purchase our 1951 Hudson, putting down a deposit of one hundred and twenty-five dollars. We purchased the car from the owner of the farm, who happened to own the Chrysler and Plymouth dealership in the nearby town of Kenbridge. This new possession became a highlight in our lives. Each one had an equal share in it because we all worked the land. With the car, we did everything together. Now, this Hudson was not a name–brand American car, like Chevy or Ford. However, we made it a prizewinning one. It was always clean and we put a muffler on it that made it sound so sweet. Needless to say, it was our pride and joy.

We discovered that the only problem with owning the vehicle involved the responsibility of maintaining and putting gas in it: at times, a seemingly insurmountable challenge. Each time the car broke down we would have to walk or borrow money to get it repaired. In the fall of 1959 we traded cars. The first trade was for a 1953 Desoto, then for a 1955 Desoto, and then for a 1957 Buick. Each year, one brother would graduate from high school. Not only would he leave home, but would also bequeath the same two acres of tobacco to the remaining brothers. By the time only two of us were left at home, things did not seem to be working out with regard to our joint ownership of a car. At this point, I told my mom and dad that I did not want to purchase another car with my older brother who was still at home. Consequently, during the fall of 1962, we turned in the car and paid off the balance. My brother graduated and departed for New Jersey. At this point, I purchased my uncle's old 1950 Chevrolet in order to have a means of transportation.

One of the most comical memories associated with our owning a car occurred one night, on our way back home from visiting some girls in another county. We stopped to use the bathroom alongside the road. When we got back in and restarted the car, we were surprised that it would not shift to drive. It was automatically in reverse because the pressure plate in the standard shifts of the 1951 Hudson had been worn out. "What do we do now?" we asked. One of us stayed in the car to push on the clutch, while the others managed to turn it around in the middle of the road. We began to push it so that it would start, and then we jumped in. At this point, we were driving in reverse for at least thirteen miles because it would not go forward. Eventually, we were able to stop at the house of family friends, where we were welcomed. While the car was stuck in reverse, we had to stop a few times because it was running hot. We allowed it to cool off and put some water in the radiator, so that we could start driving in reverse again. That experience made for a fun night. The five of us arrived home at about three o'clock in the morning.

At the age of fifteen, I got my driver's license. I already knew how to drive from having done so on the farm and from participating in driving contests through the 4-H Club. While in school, I became a substitute bus driver. I gathered a lot of driving proficiency while substituting for some of the older drivers who were otherwise occupied by their job and home on the farm. Moreover, during my last three years in school and as a member of the 4-H Club, I raised one acre of sweet potatoes, which I profitably sold to the merchants in town.

There were many ups and downs in my life during elementary and high school. I am grateful to God that the good times significantly outweighed the bad times, and that I graduated. Most of the bad times consisted of my crying because I could not go to school. I had to work or sometimes had no shoes to wear. Good times occurred when I got up in the morning and did not hear my father say, "I need you boys to stay home today." The enjoyment of learning something other than farming, being with friends at school, playing sports, engaging in outside activities related to school over weekends, or just knowing that the teachers cared about us as individuals was remarkable. I graduated from high school with about a C average on June 3, 1963. My education did not end there. I eventually attended Fisher Junior College in Boston on the G.I. Bill. I went to the Local 7 Ironworker Apprenticeship School and graduated as a journeyman ironworker and certified welder. Later, I obtained my Master in Religious Education and Doctor in Urban Ministry from Gordon-Conwell Theological Seminary. However, my first step after high school was one that I had not planned. On August 29, 1963 I went into the U.S. Navy.

My schooling and various learning experiences comprised a long and sometimes arduous journey. Many times I felt like giving it up, but somehow found strength to keep going. However, I believe that God designed it this way and that I was meant to travel this road at an older age with struggles. As a result, I was able to appreciate the adventure more as well as sharing it with others, showing them that education is still possible even for those who do not perform well academically, or who encounter teachers who claim they are incapable. As a matter of fact, I feel that these challenges motivated me and should likewise compel others to push to reach greater heights—all thanks go to God!

I honor and praise my Lord and Savior for making it possible for me to pursue and gain the education, wisdom, and experience that I have attained. There were times when some in my life said that I could not do it. To a great extent, I also believed that I could not do it. However, as I traveled on the journey, I gained a different perspective that motivated me even more. That perspective was: if anyone told me that I could not do something that was within the realm of possibility, my goal was to prove them wrong. I learned in life that with God all things are possible if you only believe. By the grace and love of God, who instilled faith in me, I kept going. To my wife and family, to the many mentors I have had, and to all others who have helped me to achieve my goals, I truly thank God for you! Amen.

CHAPTER 3

Military Life

After graduation, there was a lot of joy in my heart and many ideas in my head about what to do and where to go—but no funds to do anything. My first desire was to go to college: Virginia State College in Petersburg, Virginia. I had hoped to play football but my grades were not good enough to get into a four-year school. I then considered attending for two years to study barbering but decided against that because I truly wanted to play football. For the balance of June, July, and most of the month of August, I continued to work on a farm in the tobacco field until I became totally fed up. Since my father was in the hospital during the early part of the year and was not able to do much work, most of the work was done by my mother, my younger sisters and brothers who were home, and me. Most of the planting took place in the late spring and early summer; and during mid-July and August the harvesting began. In the early part of July my brother Danny, who had graduated the year before, came back home to stay. Within a few weeks of his return the owner of the farm and my father decided to give him the two acres of tobacco that usually went to me and my brothers. At that time, I was the only one left of the four of us who worked the crops. Also, as assurance that Danny would stay, he was given money in July to purchase a car while I had nothing. I worked and supervised the other workers that we had hired to help us on the farm— yet, when it came to harvesting the tobacco there was nothing set aside for me. This was very upsetting for me and I realized that the time had come for me to move on.

Later in life, as I understood the story of the prodigal son, I was able to better understand why my parents did what they did. All parents know that their children are different, and they knew my capabilities and knew my brother Danny as well. They gave to him what they felt was needed for him to turn his life around, and they knew that someday I would gain understanding of why they made provision for him.

On the last Thursday of August I took a trip to Petersburg, Virginia to the Army base where the military recruiters were and took tests to go into the Air Force. After taking the tests, I was informed that my score was one point below the acceptance score to enter into the Air Force. However, the recruiter stated that the Navy recruiter right down the hall would accept me if I wanted to go into the Navy. With my mind set and ready to make the move I decided to go visit with the Navy recruiter. As a result of our meeting he informed me that he could pick me up on Monday at six o'clock in the morning and by that afternoon I would be on a train heading to Great Lakes, Illinois for training.[1] I said yes, and I went home and informed my parents. They were heartbroken when I told them. However, years later my father recalled that at the time I told him that I felt I could do more for my parents if I was not at home— and that turned out to be true. Upon my leaving, my dad gave me twenty-five dollars—all I had to show for working the farm for eight months—and I was on my way. I had two days to get ready and early that Monday morning I was picked up to travel to Richmond, Virginia where we boarded the train for my first train ride.

We arrived in Chicago the next day and were bussed to the Great Lakes Training Center. We did not have time on the first day to get our sea bags so we were housed in a drill hall that night. This was a very memorable night because it was the occasion of my first nightmare. In the middle of the night I heard myself screaming and the person that was underneath me kicked my bunk and woke me up. Boot camp training was not a very easy task for someone who had never been away from home for any amount of time. Many who arrived there on the first night and for the first few weeks were trying to go "AWOL."[2] For us, the first two weeks were like being in the water and treading it but not going anywhere. The Great Lakes Center was overcrowded due to the closing of the Naval Training Center in San Diego,

1. I later discovered that the two recruiters were working together and that the Air Force recruiter had already met his quota and sent me to the Navy recruiter to help him fulfill his quota.

2. Away Without Leave

California. The building had been burned down because of an outbreak of spider meningitis.[3]

In the process of waiting around, our chief had a lot of time to interview the group and to decide who was going to be our leader. He came to me and wanted me to consider taking on that role. However, when the question of "Can you swim?" was asked the answer was "No." Therefore, I was removed from the lists because I would have to go to the swimming classes that would take up a lot of my time when the leader needed to do other things. In the second week of training, I began to take swimming classes twice a week. I remember those classes, having to jump off the tower. Not knowing how to swim, I would pray to God to deliver me and bring me out. After the third week in the shallow water I still could not swim, so I began to jump off the tower with the others. Each time I had to be pulled out by the director with a pole because I was not able to keep my head above water. Finally, after about the fourth week, the swimming director swam out to get me and placed his hand underneath my back and showed me how to stretch out and swim on my back. When doing so he noted that I had very little air in my lungs and said, "You are breathing like a piss ant." I started to breathe deeper and before I knew it he was no longer holding me up and I was swimming. Praise the Lord.

As the group was formed, I was designated to be the flagman, which meant that I did not have to go through learning the procedures for the drill march. It was my responsibility to just stand and hold the flag. I was told that I was given the job as a flagman due to my beautiful steps and struts in marching. We were in boot camp for eight weeks instead of six because of the two-week delay. About midway, we were able to get a weekend pass. On my weekend off, the Green Bay Packers were playing the Chicago Bears in Chicago so another recruit and I went to the stadium to see the Bears. We did not have tickets and we were told that the game was sold out. However, the gatekeeper instructed us to stand at the gate while he tried to get us in. He asked if we could jump over the gate entry and we said, "Yes." So he said, "When I turn my back to you, jump it and go on in: you may find a seat." We jumped the gate and went into the upper part of the stadium, found some seats, relaxed, and watched our first pro football game live in October 1963.

Due to our not starting training for two weeks, the twenty-five dollars that I had was getting very low. I did not need money to buy food or clothing, so I made it last. Training was hard and tedious, but I believe everyone

3. So called because spiders can sometimes carry the virus that leads to meningitis.

made it with the exception of two recruits who somehow got lost along the way or went "AWOL." The month of November was very difficult because the Chicago area began to get cold and this was my first experience of such a cold climate.

Because I had to go to swimming classes two and three times per week, I was not able to keep up with the training and work. For one week I was placed with another group who arrived two weeks after we started. While there, that company commander allowed me to just stay in the room and study so that I could catch up with my group. That went well, and I was able to be tested and return to my original group.

On the last week of training, we had to go through many tests, including swimming. I took my swimming tests but failed them because I was not able to tread water for five minutes. When the swimming instructor saw this, he sent me back to the barracks and said, "We have another test this afternoon: come back and try again." I would have to pass this test because graduation was the next day and the day after that we were all going home. So that afternoon, I went back to take the swimming tests again and the instructor saw who I was. When it came time to tread water he said, "Just keep swimming around the pool two times." The second time around, he said, "Get out: you got it—you can go." Praise the Lord, I was one happy sailor and I was going home.

During that week, we also received our orders as to where we were going to be stationed. I was hoping to go to the West Coast where it was warm but that did not happen. My orders were to be on the USS *Wasp* that was supposed to be stationed in Rhode Island, but at the time the ship was in Boston, Massachusetts in the dry dock. The day we left boot camp turned out to be a very sad but historic day. When we boarded the plane leaving to go home, we heard that President Kennedy had been shot. When we arrived in Washington, DC we found out that he was dead. This was a very sad day for me, for my family, and for the entire world. It went down in history as the day that the world stood still. The election of JFK gave so much hope to the African-American community and to the Civil Rights Movement. When this assassination took place it was devastating to many people who had great hopes for a major change in America. For me to arrive in Washington, DC to hear the news that he had passed away and to have to remain there in the airport until the next morning was overwhelming.

This would also mark the first time that I had traveled by plane and to this day it was the worst plane ride that I have had. I stayed in the

Washington, DC airport overnight and slept on the floor, waiting to take a twenty-three minute flight to Richmond, Virginia the next day. This did not make me feel good. However, although a thunderstorm was very bad, I did not let it bother me very much because I was so happy to be going home. Being around my family helped a great deal during the sad time of knowing that our president had been killed. Unfortunately, I had only two weeks to be at home and I spent good amount of that time helping my parents on the farm.

When my leave was over, I took my next plane ride to Rhode Island. I stayed there overnight and was then bussed to the ship in Boston. On route to Rhode Island the plane stopped in New Jersey, where I had to change and wait for the next outgoing plane. While waiting I ate in a restaurant for the first time. When I sat down, I noticed that there was some money on the table and I thought that someone had forgotten their change. So, I put it in my pocket. Later I learned after eating out a few more times that the money was left on the table for the waitress's tip. This was a learning experience for me. I had never eaten in a restaurant before and I knew nothing about tips. All I knew was that where I came from they say "finders keepers, losers weepers." It is amazing to see some of the things that we learn as we grow up that we may not have learned in the environment in which we were raised. When I got to Boston there was snow on the ground and it was cold everywhere, including the ship. When the ship was in dry dock, a good number of the rooms were not functioning well. There was very little heat in the compartment where I was assigned. So, I simply pulled off my shoes and got into bed with the balance of my clothes still on me.

My orders aboard the USS *Wasp* called for me to be an aircraft mechanic. However, since the ship was in dry dock we were told to do various jobs aboard ship. One day someone looked at my records and found that I had listed barbering as a hobby. They asked me if I would go to the barbershop and work until they could assign me to my regular division in aircraft maintenance, which at that time was in Rhode Island. After finding out that I could really cut hair there was no chance of me leaving the barbershop because the navy had a need for barbers. I spent three years and eight months doing nothing but cutting hair. I became one of the best barbers aboard ship; therefore, I had no say as to where I would cut hair. Many times I ended up in the officers' barber shop. This meant that any time the captain of the ship wanted a haircut I had to pack my tools and go to the captain's quarters to cut his hair. It also meant that when different dignitaries, like the astronauts whom we picked up, came aboard, I had to shave them and cut their hair as well.

Some may say that barbering was an easy job—but not in the navy. When the ship was at sea, the hours of operation for ship servicemen were twelve to fourteen hours a day. I would start cutting hair at eight o'clock in the morning and sometimes it would be ten o'clock at night before the shop would close. There were many days when I would cut more than one hundred heads of hair. Standing on your feet for that long in the course of one day is not an easy task and it cost me excruciating back pain. This happened many times because I was the only African-American barber aboard ship. After I worked in the officers' barbershop, I cut the hair of many African-American sailors because the other barbers were not good at cutting the hair of African Americans.

After boarding the ship, my first cruise was somewhat short. One was a shakedown cruise to Guantánamo Bay, Cuba. This is where ships go for training after they come out of dry dock. Going to Guantánamo Bay was a welcomed change after being in Boston during December 1963 in the coldest weather that I had ever experienced. The temperature underwent a shocking shift from zero to ten degrees below, to more than one hundred degrees in Guantánamo Bay. While there, we did nothing but run drills all day. My general quarters' duty was as a hot suit man, meaning that if a plane landed on the ship and was on fire, it was my duty to go and help get the pilot and crew out. The hot suit man position consisted of a full asbestos zip-up suit and helmet. Can you imagine sitting with the suit on for two hours at a time in Guantánamo, Bay Cuba, sometimes two or even three times a day?

My first long cruise took place in the month of September 1964, when we went to the Mediterranean and returned on December 18, 1964. It was during this long cruise that I made up my mind that I did not want to live alone. I was also not interested in living the life of a sailor as I had witnessed it on this cruise. Coming back to port just before Christmas, I realized the love I had for Bertha, the friend whom I met in the eighth grade. She still cared deeply about me and wrote to me daily. I purchased an engagement ring for Bertha and gave it to her for Christmas in 1964. At this time, we did not set a date for marriage but I was informed by letter that she did not want to be engaged for a long period of time. In the spring of 1965, Bertha came to Boston where the ship was stationed to live with her relatives. In midsummer, we set the date for the wedding to be on October 16, 1965. We drove back to Virginia together and were married in her parents' home.

During the early part of 1965, I had serious migraine headaches that occurred every day for a period of over six months. I went to various doctors in the navy including psychologists who tried to say that it was perhaps the prospect of getting married. A doctor even asked me if my parents and my fiancé's parents approved of the marriage. No one was able to find out what was wrong. I found that the only thing that would stop the headaches for a while was to take a BC powder and drink a Coke. This would take the pain away for about two to three hours if I lay down. As soon as I stood up, it would start again. The pain went from my left eye to my right eye. Each day while I worked, I could barely stand on my feet. When the day was over I went straight to bed. I would get up late at night to try to eat something— but as soon as I put my feet on the deck the headaches started all over again.

One day I went back to the doctor, and he said, "We will try one more pill and if this doesn't stop the headache we will have to discuss getting you out of the navy." The very next day the headaches stopped and I have never had that kind of headache again, praise the Lord. Sometimes when I looked back at this I thought to myself, "I could have just pretended that the headache was still there, and pursued being discharged on a medical condition." I am so happy that I did not try and go that way because if I had told a lie, I feel that God may have allowed the headache to return. God is a healer beyond all medicine and I believe that he healed my headaches. I just praise and give all honor and glory to God. Twenty years later when I began to have problems with my eyes, my doctor told me that he believed the loss of sight in my left eye happened during the period of the headaches. He also thought that my eye pressure went so high that it destroyed a lot of the nerves in my left eye and that is the reason why I am almost blind in that eye. There have been times when my eyeball hurt so badly that I could not touch it. During those times, the pressure in my eye would be as high as fifty to fifty-five.[4] I was given information about a doctor at the Palmer Institute and Eye Clinic in Miami, Florida. I went there, and he treated me. The doctor told me that his wife suffered from the same problem. He gave me an antibiotic to take twice a day and I have not had to deal with that high pressure problem again. I thank God for directing me there to find some-one who understood and could help to relieve those pains.

4. Normal eye pressure is between 12 and 22 millimeters mercury.

I enjoyed my life in the navy, but I really wanted to get out and do something different. After some months in the navy I started to study, and prepared to apply for the officer's candidate school. However, about halfway through the four years that I had signed up to serve in the navy, things changed. I no longer had a desire to stay in the service because I did not like leaving for months at a time while being married. The other problem was that in the ship service division it was hard to make rank. So I decided that it would be best for me to seek other means of providing for a family.

Another discouraging factor was that I still had football in my blood. The navy had a football team at the naval base in Rhode Island. After applying and being interviewed, they wanted me to come and play. I prepared myself physically and got the approval of my divisional officer. We put in a request to see the captain to be TAD (Temporary Leave of Duty) for ninety days to play football. When we met with the captain, he read the requests and his explanation was; "I'm sorry. When the captain goes to sea everybody goes to sea." At this point I could see that my chances of getting ahead in life could not depend on the navy. When the ship came to the dry dock again in the early part of 1967, I made a request to leave the barbershop and work in the laundry service. Working in the laundry, I had zero section liberty, meaning that when my work was done, I could go home every day.

This kind of liberty was given because of the amount of heat one was constantly exposed to while working in the laundry room. This gave me a chance to be off-duty a lot. When I was off, I found work to do outside of the navy, and in the end this paid off for me. The last company for which I worked prior to being discharged, offered me a full-time job as a salesperson with a car allowance. During this time, the Vietnam War was escalating and many who were due to be discharged got their service time extended. When I saw that, I was very quiet about when I was supposed to be discharged because I did not want an extension of my time in the navy. Just about three weeks before the date that I was supposed to be discharged, the chief of my division came to me and said, "Womack, when we go back to sea I will have to put you back in the barbershop again." I said to him, "Chief, I will not be going back to sea." He looked disappointed because he had not realized that I was going to be in the service for a short time.

During my time in service, I did not study the word of God or stay as close to Him as I wanted. This was a period when I neglected some of my home training. One reason for this was that attending church services aboard ship was not exciting. At one point, we did not even have a

Protestant chaplain aboard ship. While in boot camp, although I was not the leader of our group, they nevertheless depended on me and called on me nightly for our evening prayer at taps.

On August 27, 1967, I was honorably discharged from the navy in good health at the rank of third class ship serviceman petty officer. I made a vow to God upon my discharge while walking off of the ship. That vow was, "Thank You Lord. I will never bother you again with praying that you will take care of me while on a ship on the water." I have kept this vow because I have never boarded another ship with the intention of traveling on water.

Years after being discharged I had dreams of being back in the navy, and was very happy when I woke up to see that I was home in bed. There were also times when I dreamed that I returned to the navy as a chaplain; perhaps that was because I knew that there was a great need for more chaplains in the armed services. With those dreams, I believe that God was calling me to be in the ministry.

I praise God and honor Him for the experience of being in the armed services. Not only did it help me to grow up and become a strong person in the Lord, but it also helped me to know that I wanted to always be close to my family. The experience of being around men who had many bad habits and bad attitudes that led them in the wrong direction convinced me that I wanted no part of that in my life. My navy life made me stronger in my prayers and in my walk with the Lord. I was on an aircraft carrier. When you are out at sea and storms come up and the waves are higher than the ship—you must pray. These experiences helped me with the storms of life. When we know that waves are coming we need to pray to God—not so much to take the storm away, but to help us to weather the storm. I am grateful to God for what He allowed me to see during my time in service. I am also grateful for what God brought me through in order to deliver me to my rightful place in life: the place he designed for me before I was born.

After all that God had brought me through, I now decided to venture upon another route. Upon leaving the navy, the G. I. Bill made it possible for me to enroll in Fisher Junior College, located in Boston, Massachusetts. I attended night classes for two years while I worked.

Upon leaving the Navy I still had football in my blood and on my mind. I found out about the Atlantic Coast Football League that had a team in Lowell, Massachusetts. The name of the team was the Lowell Giants and they were affiliated with the Boston Patriots, who are now the New England Patriots. I tried out for the team during the summer of 1968, and played three games into the season. However, my knee was injured when I was clipped from behind. This ended my football career because the players were only paid one hundred dollars per game; I had to have a good job because our first child had just been born. I could not work all day, practice in the evenings, and play games on the weekend, especially with the injury.

The year that I played was the year that Tom Dempsey began his career with the Lowell Giants. He went on to become a kicker for the Patriots. Later in life he set a record for kicking the longest field goal of sixty-three yards. That record held true for many years. It was a joy to have the opportunity to play for a professional team. One thing that surprised was the amount of playing time. When I played in high school, we played the entire forty-eight minutes, both offense and defense.[5] In playing professionally I was surprised to learn that a player only plays offense or defense, and at times only on special teams. The experience made me realize that if I had been able to go to college I might have been a great player. But I have no regrets: I believe that God had an outline for my life and that it was not to play professional football. So, I think that I can thank Captain Conyers of the USS *Wasp* for not allowing me to go and play football with the navy team in Rhode Island in 1966.

5. A football game consists of four twelve-minute quarters for a total of forty-eight minutes.

CHAPTER 4

My Family Life

When my wife Bertha and I met in the eighth grade, we were both in the homeroom of Mrs. Annie Sue Homes. For some reason we caught each other's eye and a bond took place. Bertha was a very small person weighing about one hundred and fifteen pounds, and I was a somewhat larger person weighing about two hundred and two pounds and standing at about six feet tall. Our courtship started on the school grounds, mostly at the beginning of the ninth grade, and moved forward as the years went by. Our courtship and dating only took place on the school campus because Bertha was not allowed to date at her home or to receive friends in her home. These rules created some problems for us, and some separation in our relationship because there were a few other young ladies who were pushing me to be involved with them. This was very upsetting to Bertha and I did not feel good about it myself. I suppose this is what we call peer pressure in school. I felt this kind of pressure from both male and female friends. However, there is a strange thing about love: you can go away but you always return.

Being a fairly large person and somewhat of a football star in high school, I dated young ladies in both my school and another school. However, in the midst of all the high school dating and relationships—Bertha prevailed. There were occasions in the eleventh and twelfth grades when I would take a chance and just stop by her home. We would sit and talk for a while. I finally pulled together enough nerve to ask her mother if I could take her and her sister to a basketball game. Of course the answer was a flat "No." Behind that "No" was a statement saying that I was wasting my time coming there. All I could think to say was "Yes-ma'am" and "Thank you." I stayed away for a while, and then would go back again. I was not trying to be a bad person. Bertha told me to come back and I wanted to go back. I had built up enough nerve to do so. I do not know how I did it but I kept returning. I am sure that love had something to do with it. I should also mention that during those days we did not have a telephone, so it was not possible to talk together other than during our encounters at school. There was one day when we broke one of the rules in school. As we were headed to the library together we stopped and looked around and, seeing no one in the vicinity, we landed our first kiss. I am sure this surprised both of us at the time, but it was something that we had wanted to do for a long time. After this moment our bond strengthened, and we still remember that day. There was still no chance of us going out: in fact, we did not go out on dates until we had finished high school and when I had come back home from the navy boot camp.

While I was in service at boot camp, Bertha wrote to me every day. After praying and praying, the Lord let me know that she was the person whom I should pursue to be my wife. After we became engaged at Christmas in 1964, Bertha informed me that she did not want to have a long engagement. This meant that she wanted to leave home as soon as possible. She had relatives in Boston where I was stationed on the USS *Wasp*. This became our home base. We discussed the possibility of Bertha coming to Boston to live with her aunt and uncle. She agreed to do that—and with that decision, her mother traveled with her to Boston. At this juncture, in the early spring, we set the date for the wedding, which was October 16, 1965.

We drove home to Virginia together a few days before our wedding. The ceremony took place at her parents' home. This was followed by the wedding reception, which was basically a night–out at Steve's Place, located in the town of Keysville, Virginia. The first night we spent together took place in my parents' home, where we slept on a sofa bed. Her mother offered to have us stay at her home the following night, but we felt it was time to move out on our own. It has now been fifty years and we are still together.

On the Monday following our wedding, I received a telegram from the navy telling me to report back to ship immediately because it would be leaving port in seven days. The next day Bertha and I headed back to

Boston, where we stayed in a motel for a couple of days while we searched for a place to live.

The ship went out to sea. It was a short trip, so my wife stayed with her aunt and uncle until I returned and we were able to move into our first home. This apartment was located in a housing project at 275 Curwin Circle in Lynn, Massachusetts. First, we found a place in Malden, Massachusetts, but when we showed up we were told it was already rented.[1] We lived in a one-bedroom apartment at 275 Curwin Circle for about nine months. Later, we moved to a two-bedroom apartment at 279 Curwin Circle. For a period of time, there were friends who stayed with us, so that my wife would not be alone while I was out at sea. They were both friends from high school, and one friend was also in the navy station in Rhode Island.

I am sure that my reason for not doing a second tour of duty in the navy was that I was married and I did not want my wife to be alone at home. After my tour of duty ended in August 1967, I was hired as a traveling sales representative by a record distribution company called Record Wagon. I was the sales representative who covered all of the J.M. Fields stores and Kings department stores in New England. We bought our first new car in September 1967 as a result of the car allowance that I would be receiving in this new position—a Green Buick LeSabre. In December, we purchased our first home at 24 Hathaway Street in Lynn. We had to borrow five hundred dollars to help with our down payment. We tried to move quickly because we knew that the housing authority noted that I was no longer in the military. That meant that our rent was going to go up and we did not want to pay more than the thirty-eight dollars per month that we were already paying.

We moved on December 12, 1967. That night my wife conceived our first child, Tonya. We became the proud parents of a daughter on August 19, 1968. On March 12, 1970, while we were still living on Hathaway Street in Lynn, our second child was born: John Jr. In 1971 we purchased the house next to us at 26 Hathaway Street. I was working as an ironworker and had a good part-time job. We were doing well financially at that point and knew that rental income would help as well. So, we moved into 26 Hathaway and rented out the property at 24 Hathaway Street.

On December 29, 1972 our third child, Monica, was born. After that my wife said, "That is it, no more children." I was hoping for four or five

---

1. Later, we found out that in fact the apartment was not already rented; rather the color of our skin caused the landlord to change his mind about renting to us.

more. I grew up with a large family so that was all I knew—plus, having a large family was fun. My wife was working in Boston for Sears Roebuck catalog store in Brookline. When she went on maternity leave to have our first child, we made a conscious decision that she would not work anymore. The dream and vow that I had made to God after seeing what my mother went through on the farm—working and taking care of the family while she was pregnant—came to pass. Bertha and I decided that, if I had to work two or three jobs I would do so, in order for our children to be reared properly while not having babysitters.

In 1973, we moved to 53 Gallows Road in Salem, Massachusetts. This move was one of our most difficult ones, but we made it happen. The house we purchased was a model house when the development started. We had looked at it then but we were not able to purchase it. After a few years went by we began looking again and the same house was for sale. It was difficult pulling together the finances but with God's help we succeeded. We sold both houses that we had in Lynn to help obtain the funds needed. As I understand, when we moved to Salem, there was a neighbor next door who started a petition to try to keep us from moving into the neighborhood for the simple fact that we were African Americans. We found out later that this person worked for the Federal Government at the Veterans' Administration. We could not imagine that in 1972 there were still those who worked for the Federal Government, assisting veterans who served our country, who felt the need to discriminate. Our motivation for this move had a great deal to do with what I had gone through during my childhood. My parents moved a number of times and I attended four different schools before fourth grade. At this point I wanted to move to a place with a good school system so that our children would not have to worry about moving again and again, until they finished school. We lived in Salem for twelve years and Tonya, our oldest daughter, graduated from Salem High School.

The same year that Tonya graduated from high school, 1986, we moved to Boxford, Massachusetts. When I recall that move and consider its positive and negative aspects, I am still not sure that we made the correct decision. Monica and John Jr. had to change schools. I did not know, until much later, about the difficult things that Monica went through by making that change. John seemed to have been alright due to the fact that he played sports and was a good player. He played basketball in high school, and he had a lot of attention directed towards him. I am sure that the most difficult part for both of them was the absence of other African-American faces at school. Making friends and fitting in became a major problem for Monica.

On the other hand, the move to Boxford was satisfying to us because it was our dream home. It was a big house on six acres of land, and most of the house was custom-built. This was an eight-thousand square foot home, which included the basement and a three-car attached garage; later, we added a three-car unattached garage. During our time there we were a host family for the ABC school program in Topsfield, Massachusetts. This was a program where Topsfield recruited minority students from the inner city to attend their school program, with the hope of gaining a better education. We were the host family for two of those students who lived with us on weekends and sometimes one day during the week. This was our way of trying to assist those students who were away from home. We enjoyed doing so and the students became close friends to our children as well. Our home in Boxford was beautiful. We loved it very much, but when all the children left to go to college, it became too large for two people. The other thing that happened and that prompted us to move occurred one day around noontime when I was outside resting on the sun porch. It dawned on me that I had never been in that spot of the house before, at that time of the day. When I mentioned this to Bertha, the ensuing discussion prompted us to understand that we had been working all the time to pay the bank mortgage. It made no sense to keep doing all the work while not being able to enjoy the home. This meant to us that we were simply working for the bank.

Family life for me and my wife was very important. We wanted to raise our children in the fear and admiration of God. We were proud parents and we wanted our children to have the best that we could offer them without doing anything wrong in order to accomplish our goals. My wife wanted to help me as much as possible to earn a living, but we also recognized that our children needed one of us to be around as much as possible. There were times when I worked as many as three different jobs. For example, at one point I was employed as an ironworker, while also working part-time as a cleaning supervisor, and doing contract cleaning on my own.[2] Many times on Friday evenings, if I was not able to go home, my son, John Jr., came out with me to my part-time job. However, most of the time I did not do my contract cleaning job on Friday evenings. My family agreed because they could come and help me get it done on Saturday mornings or after church on Sunday afternoons. For the most part, we made it financially on very

2. The full story of my business life will be discussed in Chapter 6.

little. We utilized all that we had and worked together to make ends meet and tried to get ahead as a family. Once, early in our marriage, we did not have food in the house and I went to the neighborhood store. I did not really know the owner, but I asked for credit to buy some groceries and he allowed me to have it. God is so good. When I look back over my life I can see many times that God provided for us in many unexpected ways. His provision brought us through many trials and tribulations when we could not see our way.

It was interesting and amazing to know how some people felt about us. They thought that we had so much but they did not know what we had to go through as a family to obtain it. Truly, it was not about education or being in the right place at the right time, nor how much money we had. For us, it was the grace of God and how he had delivered us through His love and mercy. I believe our training at home guided us and gave us the ability to train our children as well. When I was growing up, we always prayed before meals and on Sundays mom always read the scriptures. After breakfast, we would study the Sunday school lesson before going to Sunday school. Bertha and I did the same with our children around the table on Sunday mornings. Each child would have to recite a Bible verse after the reading of the scripture and the prayer. It was sometimes confusing to other kids who stayed over on a Saturday night. They did not seem to understand anything that we did around the table on Sunday morning, and we had to give many of them a Bible verse to recite. Our children were fun to raise, and at the same time difficult. They were growing up during a difficult time, when things were changing. It seemed to them that we were set in the old way of doing things. Sometimes it was hard for them to understand when I compared their lives to those of my wife and me when we were growing up. In general, there was not much of a problem getting them to go to school. However, sometimes they would cry, not wanting to go, and I would tell them how I used to cry, wanting to go to school and could not.

A little story about John Jr. surprised me, and is an example of the sort of response we hoped for as we raised our children. Easter weekend was approaching and money was short—but we discussed around the table that we wanted to get the children something new to wear anyway. When we went into Ann and Hope department store we were looking for a suit for John. Out of the blue he said, "Daddy I don't need all of that; let's just get a jacket." At that time, he was about seven years old and I was pleasantly surprised to hear him make that statement. The girls were a little different as they shopped with their mother. We wanted them to look their best at all times.

As a family, we all had work to do. Each one had assigned chores. For the most part each child performed them well—with the exception of Monica, the baby, who was always trying to manipulate her way out of things. She became the spokesperson for the other two; whenever they decided they wanted to do something she would be the one they sent to ask for permission. They were all good kids, but as parents, we had to let them know that we were always one step ahead of them.

My wife learned to drive at the age of twenty-five. While attending driving school, we found that both of us having the ability to drive was a good solution for avoiding confusion between the two of us. It helped a lot because she could go shopping and I could stay home with the kids. After working two or three jobs I needed the rest, but most of all Bertha needed a break from the children. Our three children all went to the same nursery school in Salem, which was Young World Nursery School. In elementary school they all had some extracurricular activities in which they were involved. Tonya took up music lessons in order to learn to play the guitar, while John Jr. and Monica played sports, such as little league baseball and some basketball. When all three children were in public school all day, Bertha attended college at Salem State College. Four years later, she graduated with her degree in Early Childhood Education.

When Tonya turned fifteen, she wanted to learn how to drive. One day after getting her learner's permit, we were driving to church and Tonya was supposed to make a right turn at a dead-end street. Instead, she was headed right for a pole. I caught the steering wheel just in time to make the turn before hitting the pole. Another story symbolic of my family values took place one morning while I was in my business office. I received a phone call from my brother, who lived in Lynn. He worked as a firefighter there. He asked me if my daughter, Tonya, was supposed to be in school; I said, "Yes." He said, "I just saw her in the Commons in Lynn." I asked him to go back to where she was and to stay with her: I was on my way. I picked her up, and asked her why she was there and why she was cutting class. I did not fuss: I simply took her to school and walked her to the principal's office. I told the principal that she had cut class and that he needed to punish her in the way that he would punish any other student who cut class. The principal looked at me with amazement, and said, "I have known no other parents to do this. Most parents would take their children home and write an excuse letter for them and send it the next day." I said, "No, she needs to be punished." I left and went back to work. I believe that this was showing love, and at this point in her life I am sure she would say the same. We need to always do the right thing for our children and our families. As the children grew older they understood that we did these things for their well-being. Tonya has turned out to be a wonderful and respectful young lady.

We spent a lot of time as a family traveling back and forth to Virginia, New Jersey, and New York, visiting family. Family was very important to us; to this day, each of the children see it in the same way and we all stay in touch. The children still enjoy visiting family members. One very important way that we shared time together as a family came through our RV travels. We became interested in camping long before we were able to afford it. Our first experience of camping was in a pick-up truck that had a cab on it, and we traveled to various places with the children. During this time, we recognized camping life as something we wanted to continue to do.

The beginning of our camping career came after I had a close call with death while working as an ironworker on the Mystic Tobin Bridge in Boston. I was working over ninety feet in the air out of a crane bucket. The crane bucket was lowered down to the ground by its hoisting cable as it was built to do. I got out of the bucket and into another crane bucket close by. A few moments later, two other gentlemen got into the crane bucket that I had just left. About forty-five minutes later, at lunchtime, we were lowered down in the bucket for lunch and the crane that I had just left was lowered down as well. The crane cable broke and threw those two gentlemen to their deaths. I stood watching them as they went down.

Needless to say, this was a scary situation that bothered me quite a bit. Just about a month later, I decided that we needed to take a vacation. This was right around Christmas time and the children were going to be out of school, so we rented a camper/R.V. from a friend. We visited our family in the South and also took the children to Disney World. For three weeks we enjoyed our first real vacation in life: camping at camp sites and at Disney World, and enjoying our families as we went throughout the southern states.

In 1979 we purchased our first camper/RV, which was a twenty-one foot Trans Van. Our longest trip in the Trans Van was to Québec, Canada with other friends who traveled with us. In 1982 we purchased a larger RV and in the summer of 1983 we took our first major RV trip. We chose this time because it would perhaps be the last time that we would be able to convince the children to travel with us for any period of time, our oldest daughter having just turned fourteen. This was a two-month trip and it was a wonderful time of traveling with our entire family being together.

Our RV journey took us all across the country: through the southern states, to the Grand Canyon, the Hoover Dam, Las Vegas, San Francisco, Salt Lake City, Chicago, and finally on to Buffalo, New York and back home to Boston. To give just one of the highlights of this trip: the view of Salt Lake City was remarkable because it was the year of a big flood. When looking down from the mountaintops, the city looked white. When we arrived at the peak of the mountain and looked down, it was overwhelming and unlike anything that we had seen before. Everything was white: it appeared as though we were floating in space until we came to an understanding of what this phenomenon was and what had happened to cause it. When the floods receded, salt remained behind, giving everything a striking white appearance.

We traveled through the southern states many times, visiting family. As the years passed, we continued to use the motor home at camp sites, but it was used primarily for traveling back and forth from Boston to the South for various family reunions and church affairs. When the children graduated high school they all attended college in Virginia, and we took each of them to campus in the RV when they began their college careers. I am also grateful to God that I was able to fulfill my mother's request to visit her brother in New Jersey before he died. We traveled to Virginia to pick her up in the RV because she was not in a condition to take a long car journey.

Needless to say, during all our traveling and camping, we found very few African Americans on the road in RVs or at camp sites. For the most part, it was somewhat of a lonely road when it came to meeting other African Americans. However, somehow it worked out that we were in Florida during the time of the RV Super Show at the Tampa Fairground and we were able to go. During our time at the Super Show, we met another African-American couple by the names of Delores and Louis Perry from Flint, Michigan. We began a conversation about how there were not many African-American RVers; at that point we were informed about the National African American RV Association. Our next camping trip was the first week in June when we traveled to Hampton, Virginia for the Baptist Ministers' Conference. We parked in the parking lot of Hampton University and were spotted by another NAARVA member, Rev. Wilton Blake, who inspired us and talked to us about joining NAARVA. After these encounters with the Perrys and Rev. Blake, we joined the NAARVA.

We attended our first rally of the NAARVA Organization in 1997 in Mansfield, Ohio. I was asked to preach at that gathering and did so on Sunday morning. We were amazed at the number of African-American people who were there and the number of RVers who could come together and have such an enjoyable time. We met people from all across the country. I recall the sermon very well: I talked to the African-American RVers about "Moving from Success to Significance." I had done this sermon a number of times when people talked to me about being in the business world and going into the ministry. I shared with the African-American RVers that all of them must have been successful in order to have an RV. Now that we were successful in that phase of life, God wanted us to use that which He had given us not only to be successful but to use it significantly. We were called to move from success to doing significant things in our community and in our world. One way to do this was to serve as models to young and old African Americans across the country, inspiring them to be a part of God's kingdom and of NAARVA. Eventually, I served as chaplain, vice president, and president of NAARVA.

We are grateful to God for allowing us to be a part of NAARVA, and for giving us the opportunity to enjoy the beauty of this earth and the country that He has placed before us. Moreover, by allowing us to become involved in RVing, God changed our perceptions about life: RV camping introduced us to a new world that we had not seen or ever enjoyed before. We are also thankful for our RV friends, and the people we have met throughout the years on the road who have really changed our lives. I pray that we will continue to be a positive influence on the lives of the many people we have met. In our travels, we have tried to live our lives as Christians, and to dialogue with others about the life and work of Jesus Christ. We made every effort to be witnesses of God's love and to evangelize in order to bring others a little closer to Him. Had it not been for camping and RVing, there would have been many places that we would have never seen, and many people whom we would never met. There have been many situations in which I have been able to share the love of God and do the kind of evangelism that He called me to do while fulfilling my role as pastor of the Metropolitan Baptist Church in Dorchester, Massachusetts for eighteen years.[3] We still enjoy camping and RVing. This is our hobby and our get-away and something we

3. My call to the pastorate and years as a minister will be discussed in Chapter 8.

love to do. Again, we are grateful to God for this kind of experience. We are pleased to acknowledge that God has allowed us to travel in the RV to every drivable state in the USA except for North Dakota and Alaska.

RVing may prove to be part of the continuing ministry to which God has called me. To have an RV and travel the roads in the South, means that I could enter small towns and cities and meet young men and women who perhaps have dropped out of school or cannot go on to college. It might be possible to find some who feel left out of life, thinking that nothing remains for them to do. A goal of such RV travels would be to cheer them up, and introduce them to our Lord and Savior who owns all the cattle on the hill and is able to provide for each of us regardless of what our situation might be. Education is not only a matter of academics. God uses many means to teach us about His love and care, and how He has something for each of us to do in life that will take us to another level of understanding who He is.

In 1986, Tonya finished high school in Salem, and in the fall attended Hampton University in Hampton, Virginia. John finished high school in 1988 and attended Virginia University in Richmond. Monica finished school the following year and attended Virginia University in Richmond also. One year, all three were in college at the same time so we had three tuitions to pay. We praise God for the ability to do so; when they completed their schooling, their tuition had been paid for. Hallelujah and all praises to our Lord and Savior.

When Tonya finished college she came home and worked in the family business, JJS Services, for a while. After that, she worked for an accounting firm that happened to be our family business accountants. Each summer when John came home he worked in the family business. One year he ran the company car wash in Nashua, New Hampshire. After finishing school he came home and became one of the district managers for the family business. Monica completed two years at Virginia University in Richmond, and then came home and went to cosmetology school to become a beautician. Later, she had her own beauty shop in Medford, Massachusetts.

When the children returned home from college they lived with their parents for a short while and then decided that they wanted to be on their own. In 1994 we sold our Boxford home and moved into a condo in Lynnfield, Massachusetts. We lived in Lynnfield for three years and then moved to Dedham to be closer to the church that I pastored. This saved time because I did not have to drive through the traffic every day. In the year 2000, our family struggled to keep up with the living conditions, so we found a place in Boston, in the city of Dorchester: a duplex on two lots that was being constructed. We completed the construction while designing it so that we could all stay in one building. We were committed to do that for five years and then we planned to move on in our separate ways. Our oldest daughter, Tonya, achieved that and relocated to Charlotte, North Carolina in 2005. About three years later John Jr. joined her in Charlotte while my wife and I, along with Monica and our grandson, moved at the end of 2008. We rented an apartment for two years. In 2010, I was granted disability through the American Baptist Churches of Massachusetts through the MM BB disability program. The disability was granted due to malignant disabling hypertension, diabetes, and multilevel degeneration of lumbar spine L3–4 and L4–5, which caused severe back pain. In November of 2009 I became inactive and on July 8, 2010 I resigned as pastor because of the disability. During this time, my wife was also suffering from some severe back and leg pains. It had become so difficult that in many cases she could only walk about ten to twelve steps and found it almost impossible to climb stairs. We moved to our Florida home that we built in 1998 during our RVing years.

Our youngest daughter, Monica, and her son, Malik, stayed in Lynnfield until September 2012. At that point they moved to Charlotte. We are pleased that all three children are living in the same city and that they are fairly close to us here in central Florida. We enjoy getting together as much as possible. Now that we are retired, it is easy to travel without having to rush to get where we are going. Sometimes it may take a day or so to get to where they are, but we have plenty of time.

We are very proud to say and to know that our family has been close together since its conception. We are all active in church, and try to worship God daily in spirit and in truth. Tonya is an Armor Bearer for her pastor's wife at Nations Ford Community Church in Charlotte.[4] John is a trustee at Ebenezer Baptist Church in Charlotte. Monica has joined the Ebenezer Baptist Church, and our grandson Malik was baptized on the first Sunday of April, 2013. My wife and I now reside in central Florida and have joined the New Mount Zion Missionary Baptist Church in Lakeland, where we enjoy the midweek and Sunday services. We serve on two committees and I preach on some Sunday mornings when requested by the pastor.

4. Armor Bearers help to serve and support the leadership of Nations Ford Community Church.

Although none of us in the family has been without difficulties or hard times, yet God's love and mercy prevailed. With Him and through Him it has been possible for us to make it thus far. As a family, we first want to give thanks and honor to God for how He has blessed and directed our lives. We would also like to give thanks to our mothers and fathers who raised us in the fear and admonition of God. We also owe thanks to our sisters and brothers for their assistance during the time of raising our young family. There are many others who have helped us in raising our family with their counsel, kind words, or in many small ways. We believe in the old African Proverb that says, "It takes a village to raise a child." We realize that there were times when someone else could reach our children when we could not, and we thank God for you.

In 2015, we celebrated our fiftieth wedding anniversary and our oldest child is only forty-seven. We are praying to make it to fifty more years because it has been that great. As a family, we lift up holy hands and we praise God Almighty for the things He has done for us and through us. To God be the glory.

CHAPTER 5

Ten Vital Lessons for Survival and Thriving as a Black Man in America

1. *The first lesson that I learned is that I should not be afraid because of the color of my skin because God is with me. I know that I am a person that God created like every other man.*

   In order to survive and to thrive, a black man in America has to first acknowledge and accept the fact that he is somebody. When God created human beings He did not create any junk. Understanding that what we are is God's gift to us and what we make of our selves is our gift to God helped me to thrive. I learned that we need to walk with our heads up and learn all we can about how to survive in an unfriendly world. It is essential to work hard and show that we can do any job as well as anyone else. We must seek to grow so that we can be a great gift to God.

2. *I learned that in order to survive I had to take on a self-surviving, determined, and sincere attitude about myself.* You have to be sincere about wanting to live out your life to be the best that you can be. You have to have a determined mind that will not give up when faced with difficult challenges. As a black man in America, there were many challenges that I faced. I learned that I had to have faith in God, confidence in myself, and not allow those challenges to turn me around. I learned to not give up on my dreams. I had to take on the attitude of the slogan

that says "God made me black because He knew that I could handle it." With that said, I had to put my total faith in God, knowing that He would pave the way for me no matter what difficulty I was facing.

3. *I had to learn to let no one tell me that I could not do well.* To survive in America we can never accept someone telling us that because we are black we are a lower-class people and that our brains cells do not function as well as others. To thrive in America we have to understand that although God made us all different we are still a part of one body that makes up America. We do not need to act like a foot if America needs an arm, and we do not need to act like a head if America needs an eye. We can be that part of America that God created us to be, with all of the abilities and rights that everyone else has. There is something for each of us to do because we are of equal importance with anyone else in America.

4. *I learned to use reverse psychology: if someone tried to put me down, saying that I could not do something, I proved to them that I could.* In doing so we have to first understand that the word of God says: "With God all things are possible." (Matt 19:26) To survive and thrive we have to believe that. I learned to believe this scripture with all my heart, and in doing so I will never allow anyone to tell me that I cannot perform any challenge that comes before me.

5. *I learned to be patient, have faith, and wait on the Lord.* Sometimes we think that in order to survive and thrive everything has to be done on our timetable. I have learned that in many cases, it is best to wait. There have been many times when I have made quick decisions, only to learn later that they were the wrong decisions simply because I was a little impatient. Often, our feelings and the directions of the world will lead us astray because we try and keep up with earthly matters. I have learned that there are subtle things that our subconscious makes us aware of, and that usually it is the spirit of God saying: "Wait."

6. *To survive and thrive as a black man in America I had to learn to be a part of the solution and not part of the problem.* Sometimes we become part of the problem when we allow ourselves to be lowered into thinking and feeling that we are what many Americans say we are: that we are, in some sense, "less" than others. When we do that we place ourselves on a lower standard, and inevitably we begin to carry ourselves that way. We become a part of the problem and not a part of

the solution. When we look at ourselves with the stamp that America has placed on us, we are part of the problem. In doing so, I learned that we do not train our young men correctly, and many of them grow up feeling that the world is against them. To become part of the solution we have to keep telling ourselves: "I am somebody and I am as good as anyone else in this world." We can prove the truth of this by continually seeking how to learn and educate ourselves no matter what difficulties we are going through or how old we are. We can also be a part of the solution by studying the history of African America so that we can let people know that a large portion of America was built by African-American men. We should not allow our history to be lost.

7. *In order to thrive as a black man in America, I learned that I needed to use my survival skills.* In my younger days I learned about the 4-H's of the 4-H Club. Head was for better thinking, Heart for greater loyalty, Hands for better service, and Health for better living. The 4-H's have helped me a lot in life as an African-American man. I learned that I had to use my head to think things out before I proceeded to do anything. If you go with feelings all the time they have a tendency to lead you in the wrong direction. The hand part of the 4-H's helped me to learn to be unselfish and to always be willing to lend a helping hand, trying to be of some service to my fellow men. The heart part of the 4-H's has helped me to be more loyal to others—especially my wife, my family, and others with whom I am closely connected, as well as the country where I live, the United States of America. Health is the fourth 4-H, which stands for better living. I have learned to live better in order to have better health. African-American men are the recipients of many diseases that cut our lives short. In order to survive and thrive in America good health is necessary. We need to take care of ourselves physically and mentally. We need to push ourselves to get our annual physical checkups so that we can understand how the body functions and learn how to live in a healthy way.

8. *In order to survive and thrive in America, I learned to listen more than I spoke.* I have come to realize that, when I am involved in a situation with someone who feels that he or she knows it all and does all the talking, he or she is usually the one who does not know very much about anything. I believe in the phrase that states that "God gave us two ears and one mouth so that we could listen more than we talk." It's important that we listen to others because in most cases there are

those who have experienced things that we have not, and have some wisdom over and above what we think we have. I have learned that if I listen long enough some of the questions that I have will be answered.

9. *Another vital lesson learned is that, as a black man, I needed to understand that my brothers' lives do matter.* The killing of our black brothers has to stop. There are too many families left without fathers and it is causing turmoil within the black family structure. Children growing up need a mother and a father in order to have the ideal structure of the family that God created. We are seeing too many gang-related killings of our black brothers over drugs and other unnecessary reasons.

10. *A vital lesson that I have come to understand as a black man living in America is to learn to live for Christ and not for man.* If we live for Christ greater and better things will come to us. Sometimes we are too quick to judge and look for what we call justice. Living in America as black men life is not fair, but it works when we remain grounded in our faith. We will not find justice in America as black men, but if we are anchored in the Lord we will find favor with Him. I have learned that we cannot make it without God. I have learned to be in constant prayer for myself, my family, all leaders local and abroad, and for the church, that we may bring others closer to Christ.

CHAPTER 6

Entrepreneurial and Business Life

Ibelieve it is appropriate to say that my business life started at a very early age. I also believe it started out of desperation. I learned how to do creative things that would help to fulfill my specific needs. When my siblings and I walked to school, we picked up the bottles on the side of the road and sold them at the store in order to buy candy, pencils, and sometimes paper for school. I recall living on the farm during the second and third grades, when we grew peanuts and cared for our pecan trees. I sold pecans to other kids at two for a penny. At times, we had no pencils or paper, for our parents could not afford to purchase any for us. Consequently, I would trade peanuts or pecans for a used pencil or a few sheets of paper with other students. There were times when we played marbles with our peers. I had no money to buy marbles, and I would not dare ask my dad to buy them. So, we traded peanuts, pecans, and walnuts for a few marbles in order to be able to play with the other kids. We learned about bartering at an early age, but did not know what it meant. All we knew was that we were trying to get help while at the same time helping someone else.

As I entered my teen years, I was able to learn how to be an entrepreneur, or a businessman, because I assisted my father in his part-time job as a bootlegger, selling moonshine. My father made moonshine as a way to take care of his large family. Sharecropping seemed to keep us perpetually in the hole. As a result, my father learned how to become a bootlegger and moonshiner. We were told that he was the best in the county and one of the best in the state. This reputation was not always good, for as the word spread abroad, law enforcement searched for him. However, one good part about it was that the local police loved moonshine as well. While dad was away many nights making moonshine or selling it in other places, the boys were home selling it to the local passersby. At times, we would negotiate different prices for the amount that they wanted. This work was not the ideal way to become an entrepreneur, but it was a way of survival for our family and it enabled me to learn some of the techniques of business. In addition, I also learned about entrepreneurship through the 4-H Club. For about six years, I planted, raised, and cultivated one acre of sweet potatoes. We dug up the potatoes, laid them out to dry, and then washed them. When the sun was up, we would grade them by size and by their condition. We would then put the potatoes into a barn and put a lot of straw around and on top of them to keep them warm. The last few years of raising potatoes, there was an African-American family who owned their own farm and built a potato barn with heat. This was used to cure the potatoes and keep them warm at all times. With this process in place, I was able to sell bushels and half bushels of potatoes to the merchants in town.

Growing up on a farm was very helpful in terms of informal training in becoming an entrepreneur and a businessperson. Many things that we did on the farm contributed to future business thinking—such as the simple process of planting a seed in the ground and looking for that seed to multiply so that it would feed a number of people or animals. Hiring oneself out was another way to make money as well as negotiating payment at a higher rate at harvest time.

We sold many of the crops that we planted and cultivated. Tobacco was our main source of income. However, we also sold wheat, corn, hay, and many other grander products, such as fruits and vegetables. This variety of salable goods would help one to think and plan more effectively in the business world. On most of the farms where my family was employed, three or four other families also worked there. At this juncture, I learned how to cut someone's hair. The word went viral, and I would charge twenty-five cents per head. This was a way of making some spending money as well. As a whole, sharecropping seemed to be a thankless job with a series of disappointments. I had enough of this type of work.

When I got out of the navy and started to work as a salesperson, I constantly looked for ways to make more money. I worked part-time jobs as a janitor, and later became a supervisor for that cleaning company. While working there, I tried to learn everything I could. I found small tasks that needed to be done, such as floor stripping at small stores and also cleaning carpets. This pursuit of additional income was the beginning of my lifelong entrepreneurial endeavors.

My first real job came while I was an ironworker. I had a contract to clean the office of a company for which I was working. This agreement lasted about two years. One day, I went to the owner of the company and discussed how to become a foreman and start my own business. He was a very nice person and told me to wear a shirt and tie on slow days and go out to look for some jobs on my own. After thinking about that and listening to more of his advice, I did form a steel erection company with the hope that I would be able to start a business in that line of work. Some years went by and I never landed a job. Nevertheless, I had received many offers during that time. Some company leaders wanted me to front for them as a minority owner, so that they could obtain more opportunities by claiming to be a minority-owned company. For some reason, God did not allow me to carry myself in that way, or to lower myself to that standard. This kind of deceit made me realize that this line of business would not work for me.

The above notwithstanding, I continued to pursue many avenues towards running a business, such as vending machine contracting, moving companies, managing gas stations, general construction, painting houses, and many other possibilities. I was determined that I would not give up until somehow I owned my own business.

Carpet cleaning was my next real job. I went out and found prospective customers for carpet cleaning, and then I rented a machine to do the work. I did this until I was able to purchase a machine. After about six months, I borrowed nine hundred dollars from my blind uncle to purchase my own carpet-cleaning machine. Within two weeks, I paid him back; two weeks later, I purchased another carpet-cleaning machine. I pursued this line of work on my own for about two years, while still working as a supervisor for the cleaning company—which accounts for the three jobs that I worked at one time. During this period in the mid-seventies, ironwork was very slow, so I took on a fourth job on the weekends cleaning the cafeteria at Salem State College with another cleaning company. I was forced to use my own supplies, because the company I was working for was not bringing in the needed resources. In addition, that company was not paying me in a timely manner. The cafeteria manager and I discussed the problem and he decided that he would give me the appropriate compensation for the work I was doing.

At the end of the week, he asked me to whom should he make out the check, and I responded with "John's Janitorial Services." It was a quick response, and all I could think of at that time. This hasty reply remained the name of my company for the next seven years with the addition of including "Inc." to the name. After starting my own business with just a mop and a bucket, I read about this fact in the first article that appeared in the newspaper about our company.[1] While working this job at the college on weekends, my son, John Jr., who was six at the time, assisted me on Friday nights and Saturdays by putting the chairs on top of the tables while I cleaned the floors, and then replacing the chairs. He was a great help, and so were other members of my family as the business expanded. We continued to do contract cleaning at Salem State along with picking up a few more cleaning contracts as the year progressed.

As I discussed wanting to have my own business with other entrepreneurs who were part of our church family, I often heard the question: why not expand the cleaning business in which I was already involved? I am grateful for those conversations and for their encouragement to enhance what I was doing. I was only looking at the cleaning business as a way to earn some income to feed the family and pay the bills until I could find something else. These friends encouraged me to pursue the cleaning industry through the Small Business Administration and other organizations that were trying to find minority-owned companies to fulfill their federal contracting needs. I received their advice with great enthusiasm and began to pursue the goal of becoming a great entrepreneur in the cleaning industry.

My big break came one day when I was working with a roofing contractor on top of the church that we had been attending. I knew that there would be a job fair for entrepreneurs in the city of Waltham, Massachusetts that day, so I had to decide whether to stay on the roof and work all day at the rate of five dollars per hour or to come down, change my clothes, and go to the job fair. I chose the latter. As a result, I obtained my first major cleaning contract with Parker Brothers in Salem. Parker Brothers agreed to pay me every two weeks for the first six months. This arrangement made it unnecessary for us to go to the bank and apply for a loan. This first contract

---

1. See Appendix D1.

was significant for me because, two years later, Parker Brothers opened a new office and plant in Beverly and we were awarded that contract as well.

During this period, I applied to become a Salem firefighter and received approval. Consequently, I was working for the fire department while cleaning contracts were coming in rapidly. I found that I wanted to look for more jobs rather than sit around the firehouse waiting for something to do. After about two years and three months at the station, my business was growing and roughly sixty people were working for me on a part-time basis. My brother was a fireman in the city of Lynn and worked a different shift than I did, so he would supervise employees when I was working. As the business continued to grow, there was another gentleman at the Salem Fire Department who also worked a different shift. He became a supervisor to help me out as well.

By this time, I was heavily involved in the church and had become a deacon. One night, while meeting with other pastors and deacons of the American Baptist Churches, I asked for prayer for my church and business concerns. They prayed with me. When I walked out, God clearly spoke to me and said, "John, I have done what I need to do; now, it's up to you to step out in faith." The next week, I spoke with the fire chief and asked him for a leave of absence so that I could try and expand my business. We discussed it for a while, and he said that while he did not want to see me go, he would grant me the three months' leave. I left feeling happy, but two weeks later something happened in another city that caused him to change his mind. There were complaints from the city about granting leaves of absence while still wanting to hire more firefighters. He called me back in and said that he could not grant me the leave. This circumstance occurred in the month of February and I continued to work until the month of June when I took a vacation. When I came back, I gave the chief my letter of resignation stating that I was aware of others who had been granted a leave of absence in the past. This letter went to personnel in the mayor's office, and the mayor spoke with me and called the chief to tell him to grant me the leave of absence.

At this time, my business office was located in the basement of our home. During my leave of absence from the fire department, we moved to a rented office in a building in Peabody and the business quickly expanded. When the three months' leave ended, I wrote another letter of resignation to the Salem Fire Department. After it was accepted, the mayor made a statement that I was the only person he ever knew to resign their firefighting position.

I wanted the leave of absence so that I would have a backup just in case the business did not work out. When the chief rescinded his decision to grant the leave, God let me know that by asking for a backup I was not stepping out in faith. God wanted me to know that He, and He alone, was all I needed for backup: that I only needed to put my faith and trust in him. When I had realized this divine perspective, I wrote my letter of resignation. Rather than being upset with the fire chief, I thanked him for the denial that allowed me to focus on what God was saying. Sometimes we need to see that God is working through things we perceive as bad but are actually ordained to bring about our good. It may sometimes be necessary for things to go wrong in order for good to occur.

We rented the new office building for one year. At the end of that year, we formed a company with three investors and named it PMW Realty and purchased the building the next year. The company continued its growth and earned approval to become an SBA–8A contractor. This designation allowed us to solicit government cleaning contracts and have them set aside as SBA–8A projects. As we continued our growth, there was a need to borrow money. We were dealing with a local bank in Peabody. Over the phone, the representative gave a verbal promise to extend us a loan; however, when we arrived at the bank, we were denied. The main reason given was in the form of a question: "Why do you want to grow when you are doing so well?" That question did not seem to be appropriate for a bank whose purpose, in part, was to loan money for businesses to grow. We left that bank and successfully pursued a loan with a different bank.

In the process of growing the company, I set up a board of directors. The board was comprised of a diverse group of people who proved to be very helpful. It was a board that had the company's well-being at heart. Because of the company's rapid growth, we purchased the building from the PMW Realty Company, renovated it, and added on another six thousand square feet. We were the first minority company to receive a state–funded loan through the City of Peabody. By receiving this loan, we were able not only to renovate the building, but also to start a subsidiary called Peabody Paper and Industrial Supply Company. This company was formed because we had become very large with over five hundred employees and servicing contracts in six different states. This allowed us to purchase supplies and equipment at a wholesale price, while, at the same time, selling cleaning supplies to other service companies and businesses.

Getting to this point was not an easy task. It involved a great deal of hard work: long days in the office, pursuing other contracts, bidding on other jobs, and, at night, working with supervisors, training people, inspecting the work, and making sure that everything had been completed. One significant thing that I learned at this point of being a minority entrepreneur was that in order to be a good contractor in the eyes of the majority, we had to be twice as good as our competitors. Another good example of this is displayed in the movie "Men of Honor." The film is a very inspirational story about a navy master diver named Carl Brashear who was the first black man to attend and graduate from the navy diving school. Cuba Gooding Junior is the actor who portrayed Carl Brashear. For any minority who is starting a business, this fact is very hard to understand and to overcome. I praise God for giving us the strength and the ability to overcome and to become a great contractor in His eyes—making it possible for others to see all that had been accomplished through Him.

In the latter part of 1989, the janitorial business had grown to its highest peak. We were now employing a little over eight hundred full- and part-time workers in thirteen states. Most of the out-of-state contracts were with the U.S. government and federal buildings, doing shelf stocking in the commissary stores for army and air force bases. The work in the commissary stores consisted of unloading and stocking the products in the warehouse as well as cleaning the warehouse. We were pulling the products daily from the warehouse, pricing them, cleaning the store shelves, and restocking the products in the store on a daily basis. We were also responsible for cleaning the entire store, including the floors.

In addition to such physical labor, we had quarterly meetings at our company headquarters in Peabody. All managers and supervisors were required to attend. These meetings involved a full day of training and reporting. Periodically, we would have outside consultants come in to make presentations to the group. We found that assembling together in this way was very successful and rewarding for the company, as well as for all individuals who were invited to attend.

While in the early stages of the janitorial business, I attended many seminars given by Building Service Contractors of America and International (BSCAI). This association was very helpful to us and to many cleaning contractors across the world. Annual sessions of the BSCAI lasted four to five days during which we heard many professional and motivational speakers. Members were required to take classes and be tested in order to qualify for various titles and promotions within the organization. In the mid-eighties, I earned a membership as a Building Service Contractors Executive, which was the highest title it was possible to attain—just below being an officer. I served two terms on the board of directors of the organization. BSCAI was very organized and motivating for those who wanted to achieve the highest level of success in the cleaning industry.

After about three years in the cleaning industry, I was introduced to a gentleman who was a formal colonel in the army, Mr. Jerry Davis. He ran a large janitorial business in the metropolitan area of Washington, D.C. He took the time to give me a tour of his company and showed me the structure of his organization. I came away highly motivated and made a vow to achieve the same kind of success. I went back to Massachusetts and started to work. Within five years, I had achieved and exceeded that expectation. Our company continued to grow and, at our highest level, the two companies exceeded ten million dollars in sales. When I look back at this period of growth, I realize that three components were keys to the success we achieved. First, it was a matter of the motivation that resulted when I saw the living example of another African American's experience in the business world. Second, I was influenced by being in Washington, D.C., attending a minority business conference held by Congressman Parren Mitchell, one of the founders of the Congressional Black Caucus who many African Americans call the father of black business.[2] Finally, I could see that my prayers were being answered: God gave me the opportunity to be in a vibrant business atmosphere surrounded by examples of success stories. This represented a level of motivation that I had never experienced before, and it took me by surprise. When I returned home, I set new projections and goals with a new degree of determination.

There was another goal that I wanted to reach in the early 1980s. The magazine, *Black Enterprise,* was publishing the Top 100 African-American Companies in America. I set a goal for my company to become one of them and established a time frame of fifteen years to reach that goal. We were able to achieve it within a seven-year span. We were number 74 in 1989 and number 76 in 1990.

2. Congressman Parren Mitchell was a member of the U.S. House of Representatives from Maryland's 7th District from 1971 to 1987.

We found no time to rest. We wanted to continue moving forward while also doing other things in life. JJS Services Inc. also obtained the asset of a car wash in Nashua, New Hampshire and ran it for two years. In 1989, the supply company grew larger and we needed more space; we rented space in another building and subsequently moved the entire company into that building. When we moved the supply company, we utilized the former space by forming another company: Classical Foods. It started out as just a meat and deli store in that facility. Later, catering was incorporated as an aspect of our work. Soon thereafter, we purchased our first Popeye's Chicken franchise—expanding over the next five years to three franchises in the Boston area. Utilizing our meat and deli catering, we helped to supply a large variety of menu items to our Popeye's franchises.

In the mid-1990s, a strong recession occurred in the United States and, as we expected, many of the organizations that we worked for significantly cut back. For instance, if we were doing contract cleaning for an organization five days per week, we found ourselves reduced to two or three days per week. Moreover, many organizations were looking for huge reductions in our pricing. Such hard economic circumstances caused revenue in our businesses to drop. We were not making our companies' projections, and problems with the bank ensued. We had to cut back drastically. When this diminishment happened, competition became very stiff. It was difficult to do a good job when the compensation was less and performance expectations were still high.

At this point in my life, I was becoming very tired. I had answered the call to the ministry in the late 1980s and had been attending seminary for ten years at night while running three businesses. With all the heavy burdens, difficulties with banks, cost–cutting of contracts, customers not paying in a timely fashion, and so forth, I felt the need to change course. In the early 1990s, I had accepted the call to pastor a church in Boston: the Metropolitan Baptist Church in Dorchester. For me, it was a time to pray. I was in constant conversation with God regarding how to proceed. I knew that I had to follow the calling: God's work is first. I had asked God many questions about why I needed to go into the ministry. All I had ever wanted to do was to help and assist my pastor. The answer from God was that God had given me all I had asked for in the business world; now, God was asking me what I going to do in the spiritual realm. It was very hard to answer the question without saying, "Lord, I will go!"

My wife was tired of coming home exhausted because she was the manager of the Popeye's stores. I was tired of seeing her arrive home in such a condition. I subsequently approached the children about taking over and running the businesses, and they all responded negatively. I then approached my brothers who were also working in the businesses to see if they had some interest in taking them over; they responded that they had seen what I had to go through and answered in the negative as well. Continuing to pray to God, I finally pursued the avenue of selling the companies.

First, we sold off all the assets of Peabody Paper and Industrial Supply Company and closed it down. Second, we closed Classical Foods, and began to close our Popeye's Fried Chicken franchise stores. On the weekend that we closed the last Popeye's, we packed our RV and drove to Florida for two weeks. When we returned home, I continued to pastor and run JJS Services. We cleaned up the last of the Popeye's stores and left the premises for good.

JJS Services, Inc. was sold the next year to another minority company in Maryland. I negotiated a one–year time frame to stay on in a managerial capacity, guaranteeing that sales would not go down. My brother, who was the operations manager, stayed on to run that division of the Maryland company. By 1998, I was free from running businesses and was only pastoring the church—which I discovered is comparable to running two or three businesses simultaneously. My wife wanted to continue working as an entrepreneur, so we opened a clothing store in the Boston Dorchester community. She ran the store for five years and then she decided to retire.

Starting and running businesses were joys in my life. I was doing that which I had desired since my youth. It was extremely challenging. There were very scary moments, and times when I felt I had sold out my entire family to the bank. However, it was also very rewarding. We enjoyed the challenge and we had to develop a "don't-give-up" attitude. When people said to me that something could not be done: that was the big push for me to make sure that it did get done. I trusted God who said in the Bible that with him all things are possible. (Matt 19:26)

When I look back over my life as a businessperson, I give no credit to myself; rather, I give it all to God who accomplished everything. He inspired me; He gave me the energy I needed when I felt like I did not have any. He put the vision in my head and in my heart, and He placed people around me who were sincere in helping me to succeed. God gave me a wife and family who were beside me all the way. In good times and bad times, we stayed together and we persevered. I thank God for our accomplishments in business. He put us through many experiences while maintaining the togetherness of our family—that, I am sure, made it all possible.

I am eager to share what I have learned in business and in life with anyone who wants the real facts and wants to step out in faith to consider becoming an entrepreneur. I know no one wants to be in the janitorial business—and perhaps not in the food business either—but the principles of business are basically the same no matter where they are applied. The good and the bad helped us to make it. God be praised!

CHAPTER 7

Ten Vital Lessons Learned as a Successful African-American Entrepreneur

1. *The first lesson learned in becoming an entrepreneur is that I had to be persistent: try and try again.* Attempting to become an entrepreneur is not an easy task. You may fail in your first try or even in your second or third try, but you have to be persistent. I learned that failing helps you to grow and it helps you to not make the same mistakes again. I learned to never give up during difficult times, but to keep the faith and to keep saying: "I can do it, I can do it." I learned that if you fail at one business you can always try another. I also learned that if you go into a different business from the one originally planned, then you should work in a similar business and learn everything that you can about that business.

2. *The second lesson learned is that the desire to become an entrepreneur had to be embedded inside of me.* It is impossible to wake up one morning and say: "I want to go into business for myself." The thought of going into business is a long and tedious task. It is unwise to think that because you see others in business that it is a joyful and glorifying situation. Business starts first with a strong business desire embedded within your mind, body, and soul. I also learned that this can become

embedded as a result of other factors that you want to achieve. A main factor for me was to take care of my family in a decent and respectable way. Another factor for me was to set goals early in life and strive to achieve those goals. I learned that when you do this early in life, the goals will become imbedded within you and you will strive in everything that you do to accomplish those goals.

3. *The third lesson learned as an entrepreneur is that I did not always have to have a lot of funds.* I learned by trial and error that you do not always have to have a lot of funds to start a business. I learned that you need to look closely at your situation and status and determine what you can do with what you have. I had tried to start many businesses that required a lot of up-front money that I did not have. I learned to start small with little or no funds at all rather than trying to get loans from a bank. I also learned that trying to start out big can be a major hindrance because you will miss your learning curve and may lose all that you have invested. Starting big and growing too fast can cause you to be discouraged and to give up quickly.

4. *The fourth lesson learned as an African-American entrepreneur is that I had to be twice as good as my competitive majority entrepreneur.* When working for majority companies I observed how they obtained new businesses. I quickly realized that it was totally different for a minority company. I found that even when I qualified for a particular job the standards were set higher than they were for a majority applicant. I found this to be totally unfair and that double standards were being set. I also learned that in most cases minority entrepreneurs were set up to fail because they were given standards that were higher than the majority competitors. In some cases, when our company obtained certain contracts because we were the lowest bidder, we were told by contracting personnel that they were going to see to it that we failed. So I learned that I had to try harder and be twice as good as our competing contractors. This caused undue hardship, which meant more work, better equipment, and less profit. The lesson learned was to have no fear about bidding on any job, no matter what size or quality standard was set. I learned that if you go over and above the call of duty, later in life your reputation will precede you and your blessings will come.

5. *The fifth lesson learned is that being an entrepreneur is not a forty-hour per week job.* I learned that being an entrepreneur is not an easy job and it is not a job where it is possible to work set hours. Being an entrepreneur requires you to be available whenever a need arises, especially in the early stages of starting your business. I learned that even when you go home after a long day you may still have to turn around and go back to work because of some emergency. I learned that family time is sometimes neglected because of work-related situations. I learned to call on my wife and family members for help and many times their names were not on the payroll roster.

6. *The sixth lesson learned is that in order to grow I had to give up a lot.* I learned that in growing a business there is a great deal that you have to give up in order to obtain the finances that are needed for growth. Some material things that I obtained along the way had to be sold in order to maintain growth and to pay the bills. There were times when I had to give up my social life and went without a vacation for many years.

7. *The seventh lesson learned as an entrepreneur is that I had to know how to carefully interview and choose the right people for the right positions.* If this lesson is not learned the results can be very devastating. I learned how one person can destroy your entire business and dream with one mistake. I have also learned to be discreet and to follow policy manuals that are written to prevent discrimination. I learned how to detect in professional interviews those individuals who have no plans for following company procedures but just want a job to get paid.

8. *The eighth lesson learned is that once I was in business everyone thought I was rich and I was not.* It seems that because you open the door of a business the perception is that you are rich. I learned that you have to protect your little investment and learn to say no to many who come after you for freebies.

9. *The ninth lesson learned as an entrepreneur is that I always made sure that employees were paid first.* While talking with many startup entrepreneurs, and during some seminars on how to start and run a business, many new business owners or hopeful entrepreneurs think that they should pay themselves first. I have learned that the money that comes into your company is really not yours until everyone else is

paid. The work is done by the employees and the state and Federal Government requires you to pay them. The state and Federal Government do not demand that the entrepreneurs themselves get paid. I learned that it is critical to ensure that employees and all of their benefits are taken care of first. I also learned that all taxes, both state and federal, are to be paid in a timely manner. I learned that the entrepreneur/ CEO should be the last to get paid.

10. *The tenth lesson learned as an entrepreneur is that I had to watch my finances and learn how to read financial statements and balance sheets.* It is good to know how to read and understand financial and balance sheets, because the responsibility is yours if something goes wrong. I also learned that it is valuable to have an accounting firm oversee your business. It is also important to have a bookkeeper and an accountant within your company if you can afford it and the firm is large enough to require having them on staff. I also learned that it is vital to stay on top of everything that is going on within your company. I learned that you need to know and understand every little detail about your finances and financial statements. Even though you may hire financial people who graduate cum laude that does not mean that they under-stand finance and have your company's finances at heart.

CHAPTER 8

The Foolishness of God

"You Don't Have to Be a Star to Be in My Show"

My favorite scripture is 1 Cor 1:25–31:

For the foolishness of God is wiser than man's wisdom, and the weakness of God is stronger than man's strength. Brothers, think of what you were when you were called. Not many of you were wise by human standards; not many were influential; not many were of noble birth. But God chose the foolish things of the world to shame the wise; God chose the weak things of the world to shame the strong. He chose the lowly things of this world and the despised things, and the things that are not, to nullify the things that are, so that no one may boast before him. It is because of him that you are in Christ Jesus, who has become for us wisdom from God, that is, our righteousness, holiness and redemption. Therefore, as it is written; let him who boasts, boast in the Lord.

As far back as I can remember, which was about the age of four, my mother was our family's spiritual advisor. She did so by being a model mother, and a model Christian in our church and the community. I recall eating at the table in the kitchen three times a day; mom and dad had a chair at the end of the table and there were two benches on each side. We all ate together and before each meal there was prayer, giving thanks to God for the meal. The table and benches that we sat on were made by my father and when I left home at the age of nineteen they were still being used. On Sunday mornings at breakfast time, mom would read scripture and we would have prayer. After prayer everyone at the table would have to recite a Bible verse. If we did not know one, mom would teach one to us at the table. Once we learned a number of Bible verses, the first child to recite would always try to start with the shorter verses that we knew, such as "Jesus wept." (John 11:35)

On Sunday morning after breakfast, before going to Sunday school, mom would also go over the Sunday school lesson with us. The Bible class before Sunday school was sometimes very intense with constant study and reading so that we would be able to pronounce the words if we were called on to read. Mom would also make sure that we kneeled beside our beds at night to say our prayers. Our church service was only on the first Sunday of the month and communion Sunday was on the first Sunday of every quarter. When we went to church, mom would make sure that we stayed close to her, in most cases sitting right beside her. We did not necessarily want to sit next to mom because she would sometimes get happy in the spirit when the preacher was preaching and would throw her arms out, many times hitting us in the face.

The other spiritual leader in our family was Uncle Daniel. Uncle Daniel often stayed with us and arrived at our house either by walking or a friend of his would drop him off. He was an amazing person with no visible sight; once he heard your voice, he would remember you. He walked through the woods alone to get where he was going. Uncle Daniel came to visit no matter where we lived. He was my family mentor in both my early and adult life. For some reason I was drawn close to him and he to me; he said that I was different and very sincere. I became his legal guardian later in life. He was a deacon in the church, and a preacher as well. The other person who was a great spiritual influence on me as a young person was my pastor who baptized me, the Reverend Freddie Bagley, Sr. He was a great preacher and he preached in a way that even I, as a young person, could understand. I did not like to go to funerals, but this pastor handled them well. He spoke briefly—ten to fifteen minutes, straight to the point—and then closed it out.

We moved a lot, but it did not matter where we lived—mom made sure that we got to Sunday school and to church. It did not matter if dad was home to take us or not; mom made sure we got up, got dressed, had our breakfast, and made our way to Sunday school or to church. When we lived in west Dinwiddie County church was only about one mile away, in Nottoway County it was three and a half miles, in east Dinwiddie church was about five miles away, and the last place we lived, in Lunenburg County, church was seven miles from home. In all cases we walked to church on most Sundays and walked home. If it was raining mom would sometimes allow us to stay home; otherwise, we made our way out the door to church. There were times when we wanted to pray for rain. However, on most days we did not fight it and were happy to go. In many cases we knew we would meet up with friends and after service have some fun. When I began to look back at what we had to go through, I give thanks to God and to my mom for being the mother that she was: she kept us moving and motivated in a godly way.

I recall being baptized at the age of eight during revival at the Flat Rock Baptist Church in Kenbridge, Virginia in the last week of July 1952. I had to go up and sit on the first pew that was called the mourners' bench, and I was baptized on the first Sunday of August. At that time we were living in Nottoway County near Blackstone; it was a thirty mile drive to go back to Flat Rock Baptist Church.

When we moved back to Lunenburg County I was ten years old and we all began to work in the church on different committees and boards. I was a member of the usher board and my father was the president. My older brother Alphonse was a junior deacon, my brother George sang in the young adult choir. My brothers and I began to take our singing group, *The Spiritual Five* or *The Womack Brothers*, to another level. The fifth person was not our blood brother but he sang with us for a long period of time. By then, my brother Daniel had learned to play the guitar very well and he was playing for the group. As we journeyed through our teenage lives, we sang for six years together and celebrated six anniversaries with many other groups in attendance each year. What joyful times they were. There was also much happiness during the week because at least once a month three, four, or five groups would come together on a weekday evening and rehearse. These were spirit-filled and joyful times with other groups. It was also good fellowship and good eating, for the host's parent would prepare food for everyone.

One fall after harvesting the crop in 1956 or 1957, we had a fairly good year and dad drove us to Richmond to shop. We purchased matching suits to wear when we sang as a group, as well as our first electric guitar and amplifier. Those new suits and that electric guitar really made us *sang*. When my older two brothers finished high school and went away, our group broke up. I dreamed for years that someday we as brothers could come back together and sing as a group again; but that never happened, other than at our father's funeral in 2008.

My spiritual walk continued; as a teenager I stayed involved in church, in spiritual activities, and in school. I was mostly quiet and somewhat of a loner. I dreamed and prayed a great deal. I walked through the woods alone, praying and wishing for a better life for my family and myself. I was always concerned about our family life. My dad was often away, and I walked the roads hoping to hear and to see him come in while praying to God that he was okay. I am a dreamer and my favorite story in the Bible is the story of Joseph the Dreamer. I have often thought that the Joseph story and my life have some great similarities. Although this perspective may be difficult for many to understand, I believe God placed it in my heart to use Joseph's story to enlighten me as I go through life. This insight came to me later in life as I read and studied the book of Genesis. I was especially touched in seminary when we did a play on Joseph's life—and how he and his family came back together. There have not been many nights that I have not dreamed about home: home meaning where I grew up and about the life that I had there. I have endeavored to come to grips with what the dreams mean. I pray at this stage of my life that I am drawing close to the reality of their meaning.

I believe that one of the most prayerful times of my life occurred in my last year in high school. I had to make many decisions, and during the year I was faced with an awesome responsibility. During that year, my father was hospitalized with a bad back and of the ten children that mom and dad had, I was then the eldest sibling at home. There was a great deal of work to be done, as well as planning and decisions for me to make in my senior year. In addition, there were personal concerns on my heart. When I graduated from high school and made the decision to enter into the navy, it was not an ideal choice, but later I found it to be a God–sent decision. My statement to my father that I could do more for the family if I left home than if I stayed turned out to be very true: God instilled in me His love for my family. Strangely enough, I do not remember saying those words to my father; I believe that God placed them there for me and for my dad.

Prayer life in the navy continued beyond my expectations. Each night at taps, I was asked to lead the evening prayer for my group division. I had to go to the swimming classes at night, so I was not able to study our assignments as others could and that put me behind. As a result, it kept me on my knees. God continued to open doors and to make a way through the difficult times of boot camp.

After boot camp, I was assigned my tour of duty on the USS *Wasp* in Boston. My tour of duty turned out to be the weakest part of my spiritual life. Church aboard ship, compared with the church life that I had before, was close to none. I tried to read the Bible daily and was made to feel embarrassed by the troops for doing that. They always wanted to give me some alternative books to read. Once I was married and the ship was in port, my wife and I attended different churches in Boston. We finally made a church connection and joined the church in Woburn, Massachusetts where my wife's relatives attended. When I got out of service, we joined the St. John's Baptist Church in Woburn.

I have mentioned that Bertha and I wanted to raise our children as we were raised and so we began to follow the pattern of our parents. We taught our children around the breakfast table like my parents did. We always blessed the food and recited a Bible verse, and on Sunday mornings we would read scripture. We made sure that the children were in church each Sunday. During the early years at St. John's Baptist Church there was no Sunday school and so we made up our minds that we would leave and go to another church where there was Sunday school. On the last Sunday when we announced we were leaving, the area minister was there—the Rev. John Duhon, from the American Baptist Churches— and he was preaching that Sunday. He asked us to come back the next Sunday and that he would have someone there who would assist in starting a Sunday school. This did happen and we continued to go to St. John's Baptist Church for the next thirty years.

In 1975, I was asked to serve as a deacon. I said yes reluctantly simply because I was not sure that I could perform the duties and live up to the expectations. One year later, my wife Bertha was asked to serve as a deaconess, so we both served in this capacity. I was not comfortable as a deacon because I wanted to learn more about the role. I was told to join the Deacon's Union in Boston, but when I went there to join I was told that I could not do so until I was ordained. Upon being ordained I returned and was accepted; one year later I was asked to serve as their vice president. Two years later I was voted in to be the president of the Boston Deacon's Union and the Ladies Auxiliary. I served there for many years until I accepted the call to preach. In my spiritual walk and effort to continue to learn, I began taking a home study course through the American Baptist Churches. My tutor was the Reverend Arthur T. Gerald, a graduate of Gordon-Conwell Theological Seminary. We tried this for about six months and it was not working for me or for Rev. Gerald. In 1977 I heard about the evening course that was offered through Gordon-Conwell Theological Seminary on the Boston Campus; it was called CUME, which stands for Center for Urban Ministerial Education. Courses were held in the Martin Luther King House, which was part of the Twelfth Baptist Church of Boston. At the time of its conception, students were given certificates for each course completed, which would lead to credits towards a diploma or a degree.

My first course was on the book of John; the instructor was the now Bishop Samuel Hogan. In the beginning I was not interested in the credits: I was just going to learn more about the Bible—or so I thought. After taking three courses my pastor encouraged me to dig in, work hard, and accept the credits. I was taking one class a week when I started and it was not that hard because I was working at the fire department and had time to study. After resigning from the fire department to run my own business, studying became more difficult because my work hours were day and night. To be honest, I wanted to quit because the business was growing rapidly. However, I was inspired by the teaching and learning experience, and I wanted to stick with it. I prayed to God daily to give me the strength, the energy, the desire, and the love for Him to carry me through day by day. My hours during the ten years of going to night school involved rising between six and seven o'clock every morning and going to bed in the evening between half past eleven in the evening and three o'clock in the morning. When I look back over my life I do not know how I made it—surely it was God who brought me through. My father used to tell us on the farm that hard work did not hurt anybody. At the time of doing all the work—going to school, running the business, and raising our family—I was in agreement with him; but now, years later, I cannot say that he was right. However, I do not regret any of it because God was in it every step of the way.

In 1989 I accepted the call to preach while I was still in school. At that point began to understand the reasons for my studies. I used a slogan from the story of Abraham: "Going and not knowing," which is found in the book of Genesis 12:1–5. When accepting the call, I inquired as to how many more credits I needed to graduate. I found that I was only five short of having enough for my Masters in Religious Education. I did my trial sermon in 1989 and graduated in June 1990.

I really accepted the call to preach a long time before I announced it to anyone. For many years I could feel the call of God upon my life, but I constantly said no, and asked God how He could choose me. I would speak of my incompetence, such as my struggles to read and to comprehend what I read, as well as my lack of education. I believe I wanted God to understand what many others projected: that I would not become much because of my poor ability and lack of education. I recall that long before I accepted the call to the ministry, my first real sermon came to me in a dream. Right after the dream I had a small recorder on my nightstand that I used for business purposes. I got up that night and I taped the sermon. The title was a song that was recorded by Marilyn McCoo and Billy Davis, Jr. in 1978, the title of which was "You Don't Have to Be a Star (to Be in My Show)." I was allowed to speak many times as a deacon in the church and I often used this title. The texts that I used were Moses and the burning bush (Ex 3:1–15), the calling of the disciples (Matt 4:18–22), or the story of Joseph (Gen 37). Even though I spoke on a subject that came to me in a dream, it took five to seven years for me to really understand that the dream was for me. I said no to God because I did not feel that I qualified for the position of minister, but after this long period of time it dawned upon me that the sermon was relevant to my life. God was telling me that I did not have to be a star to be a part of His ministry. As the lyrics of the song continue, God told me that He did not need a superstar but would accept me as I was. God placed this secular song into my life to open my eyes to see and understand His call for me.

After understanding this for more than two years, sitting in church at St. John's, I wanted to get up at the point of the service when the invitation to discipleship was given and walk down to tell the pastor that I had accepted the call to preach. On some Sundays I was in tears, but for some reason I could not pull myself up to do it. I suppose I was like the lame man lying by the pool in Bethesda. (John 5:1–13) When the healing water started to move, the lame man wanted to get in but no one would help him. So he tried year after year until Jesus came by and asked him if he wanted to be healed. Jesus told him to pick up his mat and walk. I sat there Sunday after Sunday wanting to move and complete this burden of calling, but I kept saying "maybe next Sunday" and putting it off until I felt that I could not put it off any more.

Then one night God troubled the water in my life. I was lying in bed one night at our home in Boxford, and I had a dream about a thunderstorm.

The storm was the worst that I have ever been in or ever heard. The dream reminded me of memories from back in Virginia. When we had a thunderstorm all of us would close the door and sit together quietly. There was severe lightning and thunder, but in the dream, the storm was only over our house and nowhere else. I could see the sun shine everywhere else, but then a loud flash of lightning came as I closed the door. It seemed as though it hit my leg although I felt no pain and nothing happened. However, a voice came out of the flash of lightning and said, "John, you're not doing what I want you to do." That dream and the voice came to me over and over again. I believe it was perhaps two to three months of going through all of this before I conceded and asked God what it meant. I never mentioned this dream to my wife, my children, or my pastor. One day, I asked to meet with the pastor, and the deacon came as well and we all had dinner together. I then told them about the dream and that I was accepting the call to preach.

When I did my trial sermon I invited my family to come, including my mother and father. The only one who could not make it was my sister who lived in Arizona. The trial sermon was on a Saturday evening. At our home in Boxford, we had dinner before service and after dinner we gathered together for prayer. I asked my family to pray with me and for me as I made the commitment to be a servant of God by responding to the call to preach His word. The family members shared with me, and they were all positive and very supportive. I want to acknowledge that this was the most exciting, convincing, and spirit-filled day of my life. The major event was not about me or my trial sermon; rather, it was my father's comments. As we talked, my father made a confession and asked for forgiveness from God, his wife, and family. At this point tears were flowing and mother got happy as though she was in a worship service. However, we were in our home, and she started to scream and was shouting all over the place. It seemed as though the house was rocking and the Spirit had taken control. This was so unexpected, and yet it was so welcomed. God was moving. I look at this as being one of the greatest moments in my ministry. I believe that God in his infinite wisdom planned the date for my calling and my trial sermon so that this event of confession would take place. I am convinced that even if no other major events take place in my ministry, my call would still have been fulfilled. Glory to God, hallelujah, hallelujah.

Things did calm down enough for us to go to the trial sermon. That evening everything went well; I was confirmed. My trial sermon title was "Making Good Your Vows." The scripture text was Jonah 2:9: "But I, with a song of Thanksgiving, will sacrifice to you. What I have vowed, I will make good. Salvation comes from the Lord."

At this time we were involved in a major renovation of St. John's Baptist Church and I was the chairperson of the committee. We were out of the church for about one year, so my trial sermon took place at a sister church in Woburn. In 1990 after graduation, I was ordained by St. John's Baptist Church and the American Baptist Churches International. I continued to work under my pastor, the Reverend Larry Edmunds, and was appointed family minister. In 1992, I had many outside preaching engagements, perhaps mostly because churches knew me as president of the Deacon's Union in Boston and also as a Christian businessman. In the fall of 1992, I preached frequently at the Metropolitan Baptist Church in Dorchester because their pastor had retired. In doing so, the search committee ask if I would be interested in becoming their pastor. In December of 1992, I became the pastor elect for Metropolitan Baptist Church and was installed on the fourth Sunday of March 1993.

When I accepted the call to pastor Metropolitan Baptist Church, I was questioned by many. Some questioned me directly and some indirectly as to why I would go to an urban church that had such an unfavorable record with reference to how they treated their pastor, as well as the condition of the church. The question came from some pastors, some of whom said they were friends, and some business colleagues. Many could not understand why I would pastor a church when I was running a successful business. I have to say that I had that as a question for God as well, but what others did not know was that God had already answered my questions. The situation brought to mind the sermon that I preached to the NAARVA members: "Moving from Success to Significance." While I was running from my calling, I sometimes became tired of running. I would stop and ask God, "Why me?," and tell Him that I thought I was doing enough. I was giving my time, my energy, and lots of resources. I told God that I just wanted to help others in the ministry; since He had blessed me tremendously in the business world, I was trying to use that to help others. I would often ask: "Isn't that enough?" God answered my questions—not directly but indirectly—by simply laying heavily on my heart through His Spirit day after day. God's answer was, "Well John, haven't I blessed you by giving you everything that you asked for?" He pointed out that He had been watching me enjoy the blessings and now He said, "I want you to bless me." God said in so many words, "I have made you successful, now I want you to move from success to significance." I gained insight into an aspect of how God works: if you do not move when He wants you to move and how He wants you to move, God will stop all of your movements. He will show you who is in charge. So for me there was no alternative: I accepted the call to preach along with accepting the call to pastor. As I look back all I can do is thank God for His patience; in doing so, I now have more patience with others.

Pastoring the church was not and is not an easy assignment. I found that there were many things to be done, and that it was different than running a business, which I had been doing for years. In business, you hire people to work and if they do not perform you can let them go. In church, people come and join the church and serve in various capacities, but if they do not perform you cannot let them go. Instead, you have to love them even more and work with them to confess and accept the love of Christ.

When I was called to the ministry and to pastor, I had to acknowledge that my wife did not marry a preacher and had to understand that there were many difficulties that she had to go through as well. I like to tell people that when I informed her of my accepting the call to the ministry, we were driving along on the highway and I increased the speed of the car to about eighty or ninety mph so that she would not jump out. While this did not really happen, it shows my trepidation at sharing the news. Fortunately for me, Bertha had always been a godly woman and we were raising our children in a godly way. She acknowledged that if God was calling me, He was also calling her, as when Naomi said to Ruth: "Where you go I go." I praise God: my wife has been with me in the ups and the downs, in the good times and the bad times she has always been my strong supporter, but also good at critiquing my work. When we started pastoring, the children asked if they were expected to come with us. We said to them that they would need to make up their own minds as to whether they would come with us or stay in their home church. They came by leadership of the Holy Spirit one by one; after two years, we were all at Metropolitan Baptist Church together. Praise the Lord.

During my first seven years of pastoring I ran the business simultaneously. I found this to be very difficult because at the time, we had three separate business entities. After the third year, I began to prepare the congregation for the fact that God was leading me to just be a pastor. In doing so, I was also preparing the church for a time in the future when I would not be there. Now, as I look back, I can see how God always plans things long before we can see them. I am sure some thought differently, but yet I had to do what God had laid on my heart. I wanted them to have a congregation to which a pastor would be drawn. I wanted them to have a sanctuary in the city that was presentable, comfortable, and a true representation of our Lord and Savior Jesus Christ. I wanted them to be able to present a financial package to a pastor that would be attractive and that would take care of any needs that the pastor might have. After seven years of pastoring and loving the people, I transitioned myself from being an entrepreneur and pastor to just being a pastor. This was not an easy task, but here again God was in it and made it possible. There were many in the church who did not want to see this happen: one of the reasons was that they saw me as a giving pastor and one who was successful in business. Therefore, some assumed that they did not have to give, because they were looking to me and my family to take care of most of the church's financial needs. This is another reason that I believe God wanted us to give up the business. My family and I were strong givers. We were doing so in obedience to the Lord: not for show and not to please anyone else. God had blessed us and we were obligated to be a blessing to Him. If those who received these blessings misused them or took it the wrong way, it was their responsibility—it was on them and not the givers.

In my ministry, I believe I was a strong leader and pastor, because I loved the people and I wholeheartedly wanted to see God's blessings fall upon them. I am sure that I was not as great a preacher as some would have liked for me to be or as I would like to have been. However, I do know that I gave what God gave to me. As difficult as it was, I loved the people, all the people, and I pastored all the people the same with the love of Christ.

When we started pastoring in 1993, the congregation was small, totaling about fifty people; the building was small and needed many repairs and upgrades. At our church the parking lot was not paved, the heating system worked when it wanted to, there was no air-conditioning in the summer, and some of the pews were falling apart. Within the first two years, those needs were taken care of and God blessed us to move forward. We purchased a new heating system for the church and six months later we designed a way to get new pews in the church. We were able to put down one thousand dollars, and set up a program to pay for the new pews. We paid two hundred and seventy five dollars per month for five years and in the end they were paid for. The seventy-four member church started a fundraiser in which every person paid fifty cents to sit in the pew each week. In this way, we raised two hundred and seventy-five dollars per month and quickly paid off the balance. Over the course of the next few years, the church grew and we could see that soon there would be a need for a larger sanctuary. On the first Sunday in October 1996, the owner of the three–family house in the rear of the church was killed during the church service. When we came out, there were police officers all around who began asking questions of me and other church parishioners. There were many illegal activities going on in that house each Saturday evening. When we closed church services that Sunday it was a crime scene investigation.

Within a couple of months, I was asked if we the church would be interested in purchasing the house if it became available. Of course I said yes; however, I knew that we did not have the funds to purchase it at that time. Somehow God made a way and the church purchased the house for one dollar. There were some stipulations as to what the house could be used for, but God once again prepared the way so that this was not a problem. We were now at the point of owning a house and it was time to make plans as to how we would utilize it. In 1997, I took a short vacation and stayed at my parents' home in Virginia. God gave me a vision in a dream as to how we could start a building fund that would take care of purchasing the house as well as building a new sanctuary. I presented the vision to the church with an outline of how we would go about doing it. We presented our plan to the American Baptist Churches of Massachusetts in request of a loan. At first we were turned down; they made certain stipulations in order for the loan to be considered. Later, we presented that proposal and were approved in late 1998. We started renovating and building in 1999. While the renovation and building construction was taking place, we moved out of the church and worshiped in the Boys and Girls Club building in Dorchester. The church was completed and we moved back in late September 2000 into a totally new and expanded sanctuary with a function hall and commercial kitchen downstairs. We now had the old church renovated with offices in the front of the church and meeting rooms for different boards; upstairs we had classrooms and a fully operating computer room with computers for training. The congregation grew significantly in the next few years. The seating capacity before the renovation was about eighty and it now seats three hundred and fifty including the balcony.

In 1996, I went back to school at Gordon-Conwell Theological Seminary at the Boston CUME campus to study for my doctoral degree in urban ministry. I completed my studies and graduated in May 2000. I did my dissertation on, "The Call to the Ministry." This was done by gathering insight from a select group of African-American pastors. I did this to obtain further confirmation of my calling to preach and to pastor. I felt that I needed to do this because the more I traveled and explored other ministries, I was becoming confused. I knew that God was not the author of confusion. Writing my thesis brought considerable clarity to my understanding about the ministry, and about godly people and ungodly people bringing forth the word of God. Studying the subject of the call to ministry helped me to understand that I was where God wanted me to be. In addition to this, when I was teaching the book of Jeremiah in a series of Bible study lessons on Wednesday evenings in 1997, I received confirmation that God had prepared me to be where I was—pastoring Metropolitan Baptist Church at that given time—years before it actually happened.

The ministry in Metropolitan Baptist Church continued to grow and it was a beacon of light for the Dorchester community. We started many programs to assist the community, including a feed the hungry program, computer training, an afterschool program, and summer programs for the youth. We also implemented a tax filing program through the city of Boston. There were many other short-term seminars and programs for which the church building was used.

During my first year at Metropolitan Baptist, we implemented plans to start a tent revival. This tent revival was usually the last week in June; one of its purposes was to help bring peace to the city as schools closed for the summer. The tent revival went on for seventeen years. The Saturday prior to the week of revival, we had a community outing. We provided food for the entire community and had great fellowship with those who lived nearby. Over the course of the day, we fed over five hundred people. We had tables set up under the tent for various organizations, such as voter registration, breast cancer, blood pressure testing, and blood sugar readings for diabetes. We also had tables that gave the parishioners updated information and resources about what was going on in the city. On that day, we had workers from the Dana-Farber Cancer Society come on their mobile bus to test and screen men for prostate cancer.

In 2006, while I was pastor, I applied for the Lily Foundation Grant that allows pastors to take a sabbatical of three to six months. In late 2006, I was awarded that grant through the church for a total of forty-five thousand dollars. These funds paid for someone to come and preach while the senior pastor was away, as well as for an administrator to oversee the church during the senior pastor's absence. It also paid for transportation, lodging, and food for the pastor and the pastor's spouse while he and she were away. This grant allowed the pastor to step back from his or her duties and take some time to reflect. My wife and I started our sabbatical in early 2008 and returned to the church in June 2008. The trip took us to the southern states visiting other churches, as well as to London, England and Liberia, Africa. In Africa we visited the school that the church supported: Ricks Institute located in Virginia, Liberia. The school consists of over five hundred students and its principal is Rev. Dr. Olu Menjay. We spoke with them all, and then we spoke to individual classes during our time there. The major highlight of our visit occurred one day when we cooked lunch for the students. I made a chicken stew and Bertha made peach cobbler. The children were amazed and so happy, saying that no one had ever done this for them before. They were surprised to have meat as part of their lunch, which usually consisted of rice. It was a great sabbatical and, if possible, I recommend that pastors who qualify take the time to apply for similar opportunities: they will be blessed.

As a pastor and a minister, I had many ups and downs. I experienced a great deal of sickness that the congregation knew about—and a great deal that they did not know about. I visited my doctor, and sometimes went to the emergency room for hypertension. Often, the doctor would not let me go home because my blood pressure was so high. In the later years, I was also diagnosed as a diabetic and experienced serious back pain due to hard work down through the years, which had caused a major degeneration of a spinal disk in my back. In 2009, my doctor felt that something had to be done because not only did I have diabetes and back pain, but my hypertension was not controllable. We agreed that I should apply for disability. I had planned to retire at the age of seventy and I had four and a half years to go. Again, I found that my plans were not God's plans. The doctor wrote a letter to my church and to the American Baptist Churches disability agency. I was told that I would have to take three months off and await their decision: we did so and traveled to Florida for the winter months. I was informed in February 2010 that my disability had been approved retroactive to November 2009. With all this taking place, my wife and I asked the church and other family and friends to pray with us about what to do. The Lord led me to retire from pastoring on my sixty-sixth birthday in 2010. This was not an easy decision. It was very difficult to leave but God had placed the handwriting on the wall.

The decision to retire was made in the month of April 2010. I explained to the church that I would stay there as pastor until July 8, my birthday, but that I would not be preaching. I promised to find someone to fill the pulpit each Sunday and to assist the church in organizing the search committee to find a new pastor. We did that and an interim pastor was put in place the Sunday before I left. I celebrated with the church's seventy-fifth anniversary on the third Sunday in May 2010, which was another milestone for the church. I preached my last sermon as pastor on the first Sunday in July 2010 and retired, as planned, on July 8. We really love the people in the church and community. It was a joy to serve God in that capacity and to just be a servant for the people. I believe we gave it our all and all, meaning our love and time, our talent and resources.

Our prayer was and is: May the work that I've done speak for me.

We stayed in Boston until the middle of 2010; at the end August we moved our permanent residence to our Florida home that we built in 1998. Our commitment was to visit other churches in the area for one year and allow God to lead us to a church to join. In August 2011, we joined the New Mount Zion Missionary Baptist Church in Lakeland, Florida.

CHAPTER 9

Ten Vital Lessons Learned as a Pastor

1. *Be sure who is calling you to pastor.* I believe that one of the most critical mistakes that are made in pastoring is that sometimes we hear others calling us too, and not God. My doctoral thesis, "The Call to the Ministry," was chosen for the purpose of research, to reassure myself concerning my call to the ministry, and to further understand the call to pastor. I have learned that there are many who desire the role of a pastor, but find that they have not been called by God. There are many who are pastoring because people of great popularity in the church seek them out and prop them up to be their pastor. I have learned that many are pastors because they feel that they have great learning abilities and can remember and quote scripture well—but I am told by the word of God that Satan does that well also.

   I have learned and have seen that you cannot manipulate or fool God. His intimate wisdom is so far ahead of us and He chooses whomever He wants to pastor. We cannot call ourselves nor can we allow those who want to run things their way to call us. I have learned that we cannot allow ourselves to become franchise pastors, meaning that we take on the position of pastor because our mother or father started the church in name. I have learned that we cannot become pastors just because our parents say that they are leaving the church for us. I have come to understand clearly that it is God's church and not our church.

In understanding this, I have learned to never say "my church" as a pastor trying to identify ownership. If you want to become a pastor you need to spend a lot of time talking to and listening to God. You need to allow God to lead you every step of the way and confirm that He is calling and that it is not your voice or the voice of anyone else.

2. *The second vital lesson that I learned about pastoring is that there is a major difference between pastoring and just being a preacher.* To be a pastor you have to have a loving and caring heart for all the people. As pastors we cannot just love the people whom we feel have a high status in the church, or the people who want to be recognized because of their giving. As pastors we have to love all the people the same, knowing that there is no big "I" and no little "you," but that we are all God's children, saved by His grace. I have learned that some of us who are called to preach are not necessarily called to pastor.

   I have also learned that being called to the ministry does not necessarily mean becoming a pastor or a preacher. As pastors we have to learn and understand these things because God holds us accountable for those who are under us, who come and say they are called to the ministry. As pastors we must help those who come to us with a calling, and assist them to discern what they are being call to do. I have also learned that we cannot do this without allowing God to lead us. Within this learning experience there are those whom you cannot help, because some come with their minds made up about what they want to do. When this happens, I have learned that you have to turn it all over to God and leave it alone.

3. *The third vital lesson that I have learned as a pastor is that pastoring is hard work.* First of all, pastoring is a never ending job. It is a twenty-four-hour, seven days a week job. You never know when you going to be called to assist someone in his or her time of need. When we work in the corporate world we have set hours and we can plan our day or week. Not so as a pastor—or perhaps I should say that when we attempt to schedule our time, nine times out of ten it will change due to some kind of emergency. Pastoring is hard work because our work is never done. The word tells us that "the harvest is plentiful but the workers are few." (Matt 9:37) There are always souls to be saved, teaching to be done, service to render in the community, and preparation for the coming week. There is always a need to be a part of activities or programs so that we can inform the congregation of what is going

on within the community. It is hard work because even when a pastor does these things there are very few in the congregation who realize that the pastor is human and needs rest. Even though many within the congregation are recipients of the pastor's hard work, often very little thanks is given because the feeling is that this is what the pastor is paid to do. We fail to understand that no one is paid to work 24-7. However, I learned that if we are truly called by God, we do the work because we know that there is a reward that awaits us when we do it for the right reasons.

4. *The fourth vital lesson learned as a pastor is that preparation is very important.* As pastors we have to take time to prepare ourselves for the service of God. In making preparation, I learned that there are a lot of things we need to do to be ready for His service. Study time is very important: we cannot preach and teach God's word without studying and preparing messages for the weekly service. Preparation time for weekly services can take anywhere from four to twenty hours per week, depending on the abilities and skills of a pastor. I have also learned that part of the preparation needs to be formal education in a theological school if at all possible. Not only do we have to prepare for teaching and preaching the word, but we also have to prepare for business meetings, leadership, and other vital concerns of the various ministries in the church.

5. *The fifth vital lesson that I learned as pastor is that you cannot do it alone.* You must allow the Holy Spirit to work within you in order to perform as a pastor. Without the Holy Spirit guiding you at all times, you will find that your leadership as a pastor begins to resemble the leadership of the secular world. I have also learned that as a pastor you need a support system that will look out for you and have your back—support comprised of those who will try to help and protect you. As a pastor I have learned that a great part of the support system that you need can be found in your family. Family is vitally important and my spouse has been very supportive of me as a pastor. Without her being there I do not know how I would have made it. It just proves that God makes marriage.

6. *The sixth vital lesson learned is that we need prayer.* As a pastor I have found that there is always a need for prayer. I found myself praying to God at all times of the day. There was so much for which to pray. I

prayed for wisdom and knowledge. I prayed for good health, patience, understanding, peace, good relationships, and for God's love, grace, and mercy. I was in constant prayer for my wife and children and for their well-being. Not only was I praying but I found that I needed others to pray with me and for me. We all need to be in prayer for each other. I learned to pray almost all the time when alone, especially when driving alone.

7. *The seventh vital lesson learned is the need to trust God totally.* As a pastor I learned to fully and totally put my trust in God and not in man. I learned that when I did that, things turned for the better and God gave me insight that was totally different than my own thinking. I learned that when I totally trusted God, He opened doors that were closed in my face. When I totally trusted God He made my enemies go away. When I totally trusted God I found that He healed all my defects.

8. *The eighth vital lesson learned as pastor was to never say never.* Once I said that I would never be a preacher, and later I said that I would never be a pastor. I learned that I was wrong to say never because God is the one who is in control. He will take you through some things that will make you change your mind so that you will do what He is asking you to do. I have also learned to never say never like I did as a young and immature man. When we are young we can be very naive and we sometimes feel that we know what life is all about. As a result we often prejudge others. When we see them doing wrong things, we proclaim that we would never do the same. As I grew older and more mature I found myself doing some things that I said I would never do. As a result I learned to never say never.

9. *The ninth vital lesson is that pastoring is a lonely road to travel.* I learned that once I said yes to the Lord and became committed to doing His will, I lost a great number of those whom I thought were my friends. I learned that the deeper you involve yourself with the work that God calls you to do, the lonelier the road will become. Not only was this true for me as a pastor, but it was also a lonely road for my wife and family. When you are in the ministry there may be very few pastors or ministers who want to get close to you or befriend you. This may be due to competition and a sense of jealousy: why, I do not know. It is hard to imagine being jealous of another pastor or minister, but it

happens. I learned how to bear it and to carry out God's will in my life as best I could. In doing so I learned to love everyone more deeply, especially those who seemed to be my enemies.

10. *The tenth vital lesson is that pastors sometimes need to step away.* I learned that we are as human as everyone else in this world. Our bodies need rest and it is sometimes important to mentally step away in order to recuperate. I was deeply impressed with the book, *Rest in the Storm: Self-Care Strategies for Clergy and Other Caregivers*, by Rev. Dr. Kirk Byron Jones.[1] I learned from the example of Jesus, who took breaks to rest. If Jesus had to take breaks, who am I as a pastor to be made to feel as if I am an iron man? I learned that there are programs and grants that are given to pastors to allow them to step away from their pulpits to get rest. When I learned of this I applied for a sabbatical and it was granted. Without that I may not have been able to continue pastoring as long as I did. I learned that everybody needs rest and that God will bless you when you take care of His temple, which is your body.

---

1. Jones, *Rest in the Storm: Self-Care Strategies for Clergy and Other Caregivers.*

Community Service Experience

CHAPTER 10

Community Service Experience

One definition of community service is "the work that is performed in a designated area by an individual or organization and for which there is no expectation of compensation." When I think of community service in my life, I usually assume that it only began when I became an adult. However, as I reflect upon the definition of community service, I have come to believe that it started in my early childhood because we were not compensated for the work we did in the community.

When I consider community service in more depth, I realize that one does actually get paid. It may not be monetarily, but there is payment in other ways. For example, there is a learning experience that we gain at no charge. Moreover, service is an opportunity to meet other people and to gain relationships that could assist us in the future. There is also the hope of eternal life. We need to know that God is watching us, and sees and knows everything that we do, as well as our reasons for doing it. I see community service as a way of working on a building—shoring up a solid foundation—so that we may have an eternal home not made by human hands. Thus, I would like to define community service as an opportunity to serve others, while at the same time making a down payment on our account towards our heavenly home (assuming we are serving for the right reasons).

There were countless times when I saw my mother performing work outside of the home, and I often wondered why. She was frequently very tired, yet she saw the need to go and help others. In some cases, people

91

may look at this as being "missionary work." I suppose there was a fine line between missionary work and community service during those days. When I became a teenager and began to drive, I took my mother to places where she performed community service. Often, I frowned upon it simply because I did not understand all that she was doing. Sometimes, when I look back, I like to think that by bringing my mother to the places she needed to be I was assisting her in doing community service. However, I also understand that many times I was helping rather begrudgingly.

As teenagers, our community service work was limited, apart from what we did with mom and dad. We never had very much spare time. Between our chores at home and the work on the farm, we were busy. When I became an adult and began to work after being discharged from the military service, my community work really began.

After I started the janitorial business, I became involved with community service activities. I cleaned for nonprofit organizations without charge. One of my first involvements with community service was assisting young teenagers in the Mission Hill area of Boston by helping them to obtain part-time jobs. The Mission Hill area is a housing project and most of the people who lived there were welfare recipients. I was the supervisor working part-time for a cleaning company who had a contract with a local college in that area. I recruited and hired people from that housing area, many of whom were young teenage boys who needed work.

I will list and describe the organizations, companies, and communities for which I performed community service. I learned a great deal through this work, and was then privileged to share what I had learned with others.

Big Brothers/Big Sisters Association of Boston: 1989–2003

It was a very enjoyable and rewarding experience to be qualified to be a big brother, and to assist a young boy without a father at home in some of the ways of growing up to become a young man. It was something that I always wanted to do because I knew the need and had experienced it in my own life. I had a father, but he was often missing when it came to trying to experience life beyond working on the farm. I was a big brother to two young boys in the city of Boston. We did many things together and sometimes they stayed overnight with my family. When my son grew older, he became a big brother to a young boy as well; later on, my wife and daughter became big sisters to young girls in the city of Boston. We all enjoyed having added members to our family and sharing with them the blessings that God had bestowed upon us.

Board of Directors, Jobs for Youth in Boston: 1986–1994

This organization helped those who did not graduate from high school to get their GED and assisted them in finding jobs in the community. I worked with many of the young people in the Jobs for Youth Organization: being a mentor to them, helping them find jobs, and in some cases hiring them to work in our business. The many ways we helped people in the community were a joy to my family. This service also helped me as I spoke to other young people in high school, encouraging them not to become dropouts.

North Shore Business Association: 1984–1994

This was an organization on the North Shore of Boston that helped small businesses to find new business. It assisted with job matching by bringing together those who owned a business on the North Shore of Boston. We provided an overview of our respective companies and assessed how they might fit together with the goal of expanding our businesses by servicing each other. There was great fellowship and we met many new prospective customers.

Black Cooperative Presidents of New England: 1984–1996

I served on the board and as its president for a number of years. This organization assists minorities, including African Americans, with starting, funding, and running their own businesses. It allowed those who had started and were running a viable business to meet with those who had just started a business and needed information about how to expand it. In addition, it helped those who were anticipating starting a business but did not know how and wanted more information. We conducted seminars in various communities on how to start and run a business. We invited those who had business experience to speak for ten to twenty minutes. For example, there were lawyers, accountants, bankers, business consultants, SBA (Small Business Administration) representatives, investors, and entrepreneurs from a variety of industries involved.

I learned a great deal from this organization at the time that I was starting and growing my business. I learned about marketing, and acquired knowledge on how to obtain an SBA loan and finally became an SBA AID-A contractor. I learned how to prepare our financial statements and how to make a presentation to the bank for loans. One cannot place a value on the knowledge that one receives from these types of seminars. Simply listening to other entrepreneurs share their experiences was overwhelming and something that cannot be obtained from going to school or just reading a book. After considerable growth and experience, I became one of the speakers, one of the organizers, and later became the president of the organization.

Minority Purchasing Council of Boston and the North Shore: 1984–1994

I served on the board of the Minority Purchasing Council, which, among other things, was a match-making organization for minority businesses. There were job/business fairs where the majority businesses would come and offer the minority businesses opportunities to work with them. It was through this organization that I obtained my first major contract. The Council was the primary source for minority businesses to gain access to the real world of big business. Many minority businesses expanded their horizons by attending the job fairs of the Minority Purchasing Council. This was also a way to meet new people, some of whom were in the same line of business and were helpful to each other.

North Shore Community College Foundation: 1988–1992

This organization helps young students get into a community college where they learn fundamentals, and improve their GPA, making it possible for them to enroll in a four-year college or university. In this organization, I dealt with many of the problems that kept young people from going on to obtain a higher education. A great deal of counseling was done with young people who came from dysfunctional and disconnected family situations, and did not have the funds to obtain a higher education. At the same time, we helped them to see what was possible if they put forth the effort.

North Shore Chamber of Commerce: 1983–1995

I served on the board of this organization, which covered all the cities on Boston's North Shore. The North Shore Chamber of Commerce also provided the means by which one could be visible in the community. This organization served as a marketing entity for the cities on the North Shore of Boston. We conducted job fairs to expose businesses to the many opportunities on the North Shore with which they could collaborate.

Minority Business Enterprise Legal Defense and Education Fund, Inc.: 1986–1998

I served on the board of this organization, which was formed by the now deceased Congressman Parren Mitchell, who carried the name of the "Godfather of Minority Businesses." Congressman Mitchell was a powerful leader for minority businesses. He spoke across the country about the importance of minority business to the community, to our country, and to the world. Through Congressman Mitchell we learned how unfairly minority businesses were treated across the country. He was the greatest advocate that minority businesses have ever had. He started this organization so that it could serve as a legal defense for minority businesses. Congressman Mitchell found that when minority businesses were treated unfairly, they did not have the funds to defend their rights. This organization provided the legal representation for many small businesses. Funds were raised and donated to the Minority Business Enterprise so that they could provide for the legal representation that was needed. We had meetings in various states focused on the issues that we faced. Many minority businesses gained an opportunity to be a part of the global business world. This organization was very successful. Even today we miss the presence of Congressman Mitchell. The organization still exists and it is now headed up by the one whom Congressman Mitchell trained: Attorney Anthony Robinson.

Building Service Contractors Association International: 1982–1998

I served on the board of this organization, which was the forerunner for all building services contractors, national and international. I earned the titles of Building Service Contractors Manager (BSCM) and Building Service

Contractors Executive (BSCE). The organization was formed to represent the entire building services industry. There was and still is a week–long convention held by BSCAI each year. It offers an opportunity for all manufacturers to share with one another, as well as the opportunity to promote their businesses. We conducted workshops, hosted motivational speakers, and displayed equipment and supplies that were used in the maintenance and cleaning industry. The BSCAI was very helpful in providing everything you needed to know about the building maintenance industry. Important information would be at your fingertips at each of these conventions. We learned from each other, because many of us made presentations and gave examples of how we solved the various problems that we ran into as we performed our businesses. Each year the convention was held in different states. This offered an opportunity to travel and meet different people—and in many cases we toured their facilities or some large facility that was in that area. On one such occasion we visited the Empire State Building in New York.

Emmanuel Gospel Center in Boston: 1986–1992

I served on the board of this religious organization, which assists churches, potential theological students, and other organizations in the Boston area. This organization carries the reputation of founding the silent revival that occurred in the Boston area from 1964 to the present, as well as providing for the study and research of the revival.

Bruce Wall Ministries, Inc.: 1986–1992

This organization, of which I was a board member, was formed by Rev. Bruce Wall to assist teenagers in the city of Boston. It was founded by Bruce Wall as he departed from the Twelfth Baptist Church to do street ministry in the city of Boston. For many years Bruce Wall Ministries was housed in the skating rink in Dorchester. It was a street ministry to help cut down on the gang violence in Dorchester and Roxbury. Rev. Wall was and still is an advocate against violence in the city of Boston. Being a part of this organization helped me to understand what the young people were up against in Boston. It also helped me to understand a great deal about Boston politics, as well as the communities of Dorchester and Roxbury. I walked the streets with Rev. Wall, and prayed with him and with people on the street in their time of need and distress.

It was an enlightening experience to see someone who dedicated his life to fighting violence and exposed himself and his family to the danger that is on the streets. I was born in the country and lived in the suburbs of Boston. I came into the city to pastor and to be with the people, and I needed to learn what they were exposed to in order to be able to pastor there. It was a frightening experience in the beginning, but God gave me the strength and the faith to believe that I needed to go where He had called me to be, and a part of that was to share in the turmoil that my colleagues were involved in and trying to stop. It was a life–shaping experience. My first funeral as a pastor was of a victim of a gang violence killing. Busloads of students, and many families and friends were in attendance from all over the city of Boston and from the suburbs where the deceased had been bussed to school.

New England Advisory Council of the Federal Reserve Bank of Boston: 1990–1994

I was recommended to serve on this board by a business colleague who had previously served on the same board. I learned a lot about the Federal Reserve Bank, and how it worked in the small business community. It was an honor to serve and to attend meetings that were chaired by the president of the Federal Reserve Bank of Boston. I gleaned a great deal of knowledge about what was going on within the banking industry. Other board members and I shared with the president about what we saw was needed in the banking industries in order for small businesses to survive. We also received up-to-date information about the economy of the country that helped us to plan for the future.

Harvard Street Neighborhood Health Center in Dorchester, Massachusetts: 1989–1994

The purpose of this organization was to give medical care to people in the local community. The center provided care to young and elderly people, many of whom lived in poverty within Dorchester. Serving on this board allowed us to hear from doctors, dentists, and nurses about some of the needs and desperate situations that the people were facing, and how this organization needed more resources in order to be able to assist them. Some of the stories that were discussed were unbearable: it was all but overwhelming to know that people lived in such dire situations without the proper healthcare.

Center for Urban Ministerial Education (CUME) of Gordon-Conwell Theological Seminary: 1986–1997

I served as chairperson of the board of advisors at the request of the president of Gordon-Conwell Theological Seminary. While I was going to school at the Center for Urban Ministerial Education (CUME), the president informed me at a meeting with him that he had a job for me as soon as I finished school. CUME was an extension of Gordon-Conwell Theological Seminary in the city of Boston. Its purpose was to assist in the theological education of African Americans and other minorities in Boston. In the beginning, it focused mostly on those who were pastoring churches in the city while working a job during the day, and had not had an opportunity to complete their studies in theology.

Serving as chairperson was a major undertaking, partly because it involved dealing with the variety of personalities on the board. We had to deal with many different tasks, such as providing facilities both for housing and for the different classes. At that time, we did not have a facility where we could hold classes. The model that we presented at that time was a pilgrim model. This meant that classes would be held throughout the city of Boston in different churches and in the facilities of other nonprofit organizations. This was a challenge, but it worked, and those who became students loved the fact that they could attend classes close by in a facility within their community.

As time went by, I was asked to be the chairperson of the committee charged with finding a new facility that would house an office for the staff and hold some of the classes in the evenings. This took a lot out of me because it was very hard to find the location. When we found one, it was difficult to get other leaders to agree. After about five years of looking and getting the board of trustees of Gordon-Conwell involved, we found a facility in Roxbury in Dudley Square, which was being vacated by the radio station WILD. We were able to acquire that building and now it is the permanent headquarters for Gordon-Conwell Theological Seminary Boston.

I learned a great deal while serving on the CUME Board of Advisors and I am grateful for the experience. It was CUME that made it possible for me to attend school and get my degree. Had it not been for this organization I might not have been able to complete my education and do the other things that I had to do for the welfare of my family. There is a saying: anything worth having does not come easy. I give thanks and honor to God for making it possible for me to be a part of Gordon-Conwell Theological Seminary (CUME), for it has blessed my soul.

Gordon-Conwell Theological Seminary Board of Trustees: 1996-Present

While I was serving as the chairperson of the advisory board for Gordon-Conwell Theological Seminary, I was asked by the president of the seminary if I would consider serving on the Board of Trustees. I asked many questions about the board and what would be expected of me. I went through an orientation with some of the board members and I accepted—mostly because there was a need for more African Americans to be on the board, as well as a need for the school to place more emphasis on seeking out more African-American students. I went on the board in 1996 and have been serving now for nineteen years. In addition to being on the board, I have served on the audit committee and the committee for executive compensation. The GCTS Board of Trustees meets three times a year: in February, in May at graduation, and in October.

We have shared a great deal, and there have been many concerns related to how the school operates. I have learned about the academics of a theological school, especially as related to fundraising and what is needed for a school of this type to exist and to thrive. Of course, there have been many discussions in our meetings about increasing the number of African Americans in the school system, not only as students but the need for more African-American professors and employees on staff. I believe I was asked to serve so that there would be another pair of eyes looking at how the school could increase minority visibility, especially African Americans. I learned that what we speak and what we do are often different, for it has been very difficult to get many on the board to look through the eyes of an African American and to see the needs as we see them. We have made some strides in the right direction; yet there is more that needs to be done to achieve certain goals for African-American students that attend Gordon-Conwell Theological Seminary.

It has been an honor to serve on the board and a great learning experience. It has been a joy to serve with my colleagues that come from different walks of life—to share their experiences and their love for Christ as we all work together, trying to prepare a place for students to come and be educated theologically so that they will be able to go out into the world and do that which Christ commanded us to do in Matthew 28: preach, teach, baptize, and make disciples.

Greater Boston Deacon's Union and the Ladies Auxiliary: 1976–1988

When I heard about the Greater Boston Deacon's Union and Ladies Auxiliary, I had just become a deacon and wanted to join this organization so that I could learn more about the duties and responsibilities of a deacon. It was very difficult for me at the time to understand why the organization existed. I attended the meetings month after month, not really learning anything about the work of the deacon, but listening to how the members ran the organization. I recall spending at least forty-five minutes to an hour paying dues. After many questions and concerns about how the organization was operating, a few changes took place but little did I know that the next year they would ask me, a young deacon, to fill the position of vice president. I accepted somewhat unwillingly, but saw the need for more structure. I further believed that God had given me the ability to serve in that capacity based on the experiences He had taken me through. I was in the position of vice president for two years. I was then asked to serve as president. This was very difficult for me to accept because I was trying to go to school at night, run a sizable business, had three children in school, and was serving as chairperson of the deacon board of my church.

I learned a great deal through the organization and met many Christian people through various churches. It was a wonderful experience to serve God in this capacity. I was able to get the Deacon's Union to agree to start a six o'clock Saturday morning prayer service that continued for many years: this was a great accomplishment. When I accepted the call to be a minister and was later called to pastor, the Greater Boston Deacon's Union turned out to be a significant asset to me and to the ministry for many of the churches knew me. As the vacancy for a pastor occurred, it was easy for them and for me to be accepted in their church organization as a pastor. One of the things I learned from this is that you should always carry yourself in a godly way and people will respect you as a godly person; then, when there is a need to serve in different capacities the doors will open.

American Baptist Churches Association in New England: 1975–1979 &1993–2006

I was a member of the Board of Finance for this organization. For many years I was a part of the American Baptist Churches of New England. I served in different capacities and on different committees. I served on some committees prior to becoming a pastor, which provided an excellent opportunity to learn how the American Baptist Churches of New England operated.

Serving on the finance committee gave me a broader view of the entire organization and a better understanding of its functionality. There was also a great opportunity to work with a variety of laypeople and pastors. In all of the organizations on which I served, I learned that listening is more valuable than talking. I have heard people comment that I am basically quite calm, but they also say that when I begin to talk, the points that I make are usually thoughtful and carefully articulated. Therefore, I listen, learn, and think about what people are saying and observe what is going on around me before I try to talk.

Through serving with the American Baptist Churches of New England I learned a great deal about the different cultures that can exist within a church. I also learned that just because we are serving in particular capacities as Christian church leaders, we do not always act as Christians should act.

Serving on these boards and committees takes a considerable amount of time and energy. I discovered that people in our congregation did not understand the benefits of a pastor or a layperson serving, nor did they understand that the benefits are passed on to the church and to the community. Many times pastors and laypersons are serving outside of the four walls of the church, but when bringing that information back to the church and community they are often frowned upon. It is not uncommon to be told that the pastor should spend more time with the congregation.

My service on the board of finance of the American Baptist Churches clearly made it possible for the church that I was pastoring to be able to get a loan to rebuild our church. This was not only because of my presence on the board, but because I was then able to walk our church through the procedures that were required for a loan. The fact that the committee knew me and our church well helped them to make a positive recommendation.

Warren Bank in Peabody Massachusetts: 1987–1998

I was recommended to the bank president to become a board member by a major stockholder of the bank whom I had worked with and for in the Peabody community. It was a desire of mine to serve in this capacity, but I never thought it would be possible in my lifetime. To show how little I understood the position: I did not know that serving on the board of the bank would involve compensation. I went on the board during the time of the economic crisis in the late 1980s and early 1990s. Many banks were in trouble and Warren Bank was one of them. The circumstances were so bad that at one point there was a discussion about the compensation of the board members. I told the chairperson that I would step down in order to help the financial situation. He asked me not to do that and I was grateful because history was being made: I was the first African American to serve on that bank's board. It was not very hard to be accepted because the business that I ran was in Peabody and was, at the time, a sizable and growing business.

I served on two board committees: the audit committee and the loan committee. By serving on the loan committee I obtained my greatest knowledge of banking. In the early stages of being on this committee there were many things that I did not understand about loans that we made and loans that were turned down. There were times when I felt that the bank should have been making loans at a lower rate to businesses that were struggling rather than putting them in a higher rate category. Later, I had a better understanding of why banks handled loan applications according to certain guidelines. While running my own business, I learned more about the debt to equity ratio and how to read and understand financial statements. This helped me to run my own business as well as understand bank procedures. Being on the board of Warren Bank was a wonderful experience. I learned a great deal, and was able to help many other small businesses as they pursued bank loans.

United Baptists Convention of Massachusetts, Rhode Island, New Hampshire, and Vermont: 1998–2004

I served as vice president of *The United Baptists Convention of Massachusetts, Rhode Island, New Hampshire, and Vermont*, which consisted of African-American Baptist churches in those states. All churches were also a part of the National Baptist Convention, USA. To hold this position one had to be the pastor of a Baptist church. My duties were to assist the president in all of his duties and responsibilities. We had monthly meetings in a central location for all four states, as well as one convention a year in the month of July. At the yearly convention all the churches came together and we had business meetings, workshops, and worship services throughout the week.

One of the most difficult things about this convention occurred when we had business meetings. Some sort of controversy always arose, and, having so many pastors involved, it seemed that everyone was an expert on what was best. However, this too was a wonderful experience because I needed to know that learning things does not always come easily. Again, I found that I had to brace myself to be quiet, observe, and learn. I served for two terms under the same president because he wanted me to, but it was a relief when the second term ended. I am grateful to God for the opportunity to serve, and to learn and grow. I truly understand that if no learning is taking place then there is no growth.

National African American RV Association (NAARVA): 1996–2010

This group hosts five regions across the United States with a membership of more than two thousand. When our family started RVing we seldom saw any African Americans with an RV. It was not until 1996, when we encountered another African-American couple at the RV super show in Tampa, Florida, that we learned about NAARVA. That same year I attended the ministers' conference held at Hampton University in Hampton, Virginia each year. Here we met another gentleman who saw us in an RV and came over and talked to us about NAARVA. He told us about the next NAARVA convention, which was to be in Mansfield, Ohio. In August 1996, we attended our first NAARVA rally and I was the guest preacher for the Sunday service at the request of the NAARVA chaplain. After the first rally, I was asked to serve as chaplain from 1997 to 2005. In this capacity, I was responsible for organizing our church services for the national rally each year.

In 2004, our first VP passed away and I was asked to serve the remainder of her term; after that, I was voted in as the first VP and served a full term. In 2007, I became the president of NAARVA and served for two years. I declined to run for a second term because the requirements for carrying the organization forward in the manner that was needed were heavy. It was like pastoring two churches, and it is difficult to pastor just one. It was during my tenure as president that NAARVA purchased its first office building. We encountered considerable friction trying to do so, but it was finally agreed upon to move forward and to make the purchase.

NAARVA is a great organization and I recommend it to anyone who likes camping in an RV and fellowshipping with others who love RVing. It is like a family affair: lots of fun, lots of grill cooking and eating, and lots of traveling. There are five regions (Eastern, Southern, Northern, Central, and Western) and we have a rally each year, rotating from one region to the other. Camping is a hobby for our family, and the source of a great deal of fun and joy.

Boston Baptist Ministers Conference: 1993–2009

From 2005 to 2008 I served as president of the Boston Baptist Ministers Conference, which is an organization of African-American Baptist pastors and ministers. There were monthly meetings, usually housed in the church of the pastor who was the president of the conference. The history of this organization goes back over sixty years. Its purpose seems to have diminished over the years as many of the old pastors died and new and younger pastors often have a very different view of what the organization should be about. However, the organization was very interesting and helpful to me when I joined as a new pastor. It was a place where a pastor could bring his or her concerns to a group of older and experienced pastors and receive counsel. It was also possible for younger pastors and preachers to expound upon their preaching for there was a rotation of fifteen–minute sermons each month. This organization also dealt with many community and political issues that were raised within our churches. There was a dedicated group of ministers who constantly met with the governor and with the mayors of the cities.

What I found most disturbing about working with these organizations, and trying to provide community service, was that the church seemed to be the most difficult organization to work with in terms of coming together and agreeing on how to move forward to resolve issues. I love the church and I love being a Christian. I know the Word tells us that we will go through trials and tribulations. I am also aware that we should be happy about these trials because they help us to learn perseverance. However, the church and Christians seem to put themselves through so many uncalled for difficulties. When we do this, it can push away those who want to help and have so much to offer. As a result, many who have the ability, the desire, and the love in their hearts to help, find themselves rejected, and move on to some isolated position. I pray that the church can redefine itself and that Baptist pastors and ministers can come together again and truly make a difference in the Boston community.

While president of JJS Services and our subsidiary companies, my staff and I spearheaded many community activities, such as a drive that gave away five hundred turkeys over the course of five years to those in the Boston area who could not afford one during the Thanksgiving and Christmas holidays. We also provided food for our subsidiary companies' training meetings and workshops. While in business and as a pastor, I gave many speeches and seminars at churches and at schools. These speeches and seminars focused on spiritual inspiration, how to start and run a business, and general suggestions to young people about life and business. In addition, I have worked on many committees within the community trying to assist others as they strive for justice and to get ahead within the system.

My work in the community showed me that I can sometimes be very sensitive. I have a strong desire to help others. I believe that this desire was placed inside me as a result of growing up experiencing both want and need. It was hard for me to find help. As a result, I want to make it easy for others to find me so that I can share with them many of the blessings that God has bestowed upon me. What I have discovered is that it is not as easy as one may think—it seems that there are many who do not want to be helped, and some who make you feel as though you should just give them what they need and not show them how they can get it for themselves. Sometime I sit with a guilty conscience, feeling as though I could be sharing more of my experience as well as helping others to gain experience. However, I am sometimes made to feel as though my help is not needed or wanted. There is a great deal built up in me and I pray daily that God will show me ways to continue serving the community by sharing and giving back some of that which He has given me. I also pray that when the time comes, it will be received by others in the community in the right way.

CHAPTER 11

Experiencing Retirement Life

God Allows a Mess So That
He Can Bring Out Your Best

My retirement life has been focused primarily on one of my sermons entitled: "God Allows a Mess to Bring Out Our Best." This has now become my testimony as to how God allowed a mess in my life so that He could bring out the best in me, bringing honor to God and helping others around me.

My original plan was to retire at the age of fifty-five when our business was doing well and before I became deeply involved in the ministry. At that point God let me know that it was not time to retire yet. After being in the ministry for twenty-one years and pastoring a church for eighteen years, we sold the family business. My plan to retire was then reset for the age of seventy: the time I estimated it would take to complete the tasks at church that God had called me to pastor. For instance, in 2000 we had just renovated the entire church and added a new sanctuary with a commercial kitchen in the basement. I wanted to make sure that the church mortgage was paid off before I left. I was not able to complete that task as I had hoped. At that point, I also wanted to continue working so that I could receive the maximum amount of retirement benefits. What I learned is what I already knew: my plans were not God's plans.

In November 2009 I had to take a leave of absence from the church due to sickness. I was stricken with malignant disabling hypertension, diabetes, and multilevel degenerative deterioration of my lumbar spine L3–4 and L4–5, which caused excruciating back pain. I am sure no one really understood what I was going through except for my wife. There were many Sundays when I did not know if I would be able to make it to church or not. Often, after starting the sermon, I did not know if I would be able to complete it or not—but God made it possible.

Just a little over a year after returning from a five-month sabbatical, in November of 2009, I was told by the American Baptist Churches that in order to qualify for disability I would have to be out of work for ninety days. At that point we left Boston and went to Florida for three months to try and relax and to escape the cold winter of New England.

In the middle of February 2010 I was declared disabled to perform my work as a pastor and was granted long-term disability. The disability was through the American Baptist Churches MM BB disability program. Perhaps a lot of my sickness was stress–related, which goes with the territory of pastoring and running a business at the same time. Then, in 2008 we were hit with a bad economic crisis. All of these things led to an earlier retirement than I had planned. At the time of disability I was at the age when I could retire, so when the sickness came it simply let me know that it was time. I learned that my body was tired from all of the hard work and stress that I had allowed in my life down through the years. I believe we accomplished a lot, but we also sacrificed a lot. The way that the disability and retirement came about showed me that God was involved in making it all possible. It was time to retire but I did not feel I had accomplished all of the things that I had set out to do. I felt that I needed just four more years. But God knew best, and since I was not going to recognize the need to retire God allowed sickness in my life to guide me. Since being disabled and now totally retired I have had some time to look over my life, and to clearly see how God was and is working with me in every step that I take.

This year it will be five years and six months since I was placed on disability. This year is also exactly five years since my retirement from the pastorate. I can now see that it was time to retire so that I could get the needed rest to allow my body to recuperate. Most of the stress is gone, and my blood pressure is fairly normal with a little more than a moderate dose of medication. With some amount of dieting and exercising, I no longer take any diabetes medicine and I was just told by my doctor this summer that I am no longer a diabetic. While there are other degenerative things associated with aging that cause me considerable pain, God has enabled me to enjoy this style of life. I no longer have to get up every day and go to work with the pains that I had. I am so grateful to God for making this possible.

My testimony is that God allows a mess so that He can bring out your best. This testimony/sermon came to me about a year ago as I began to look over my life as to where God had brought me from and through. If you are looking for a scripture text for the sermon, you can use almost any of the stories in the Bible. You can start with Adam and Eve, Cain and Abel, Abraham and Sarah, Abraham and Lot, Sarah and Hagar, Jacob and Isaac, Joseph and his family, Joseph and Potiphar's wife: all in the book of Genesis. Then look to the book of Exodus: Moses's birth and his mother's placing him in the Nile River, Moses killing the Egyptian man, Moses fleeing for his life, Moses and the burning bush, the plagues of the Bible, God freeing the Israelite people, God allowing them to wander in the desert for forty years. Then there were the Hebrew children in the fiery furnace, David and Bathsheba, Daniel in the lion's den, Jonah in the belly of the whale. I am sure that you can see from the aforementioned stories in the Bible how God allowed a mess so that He could bring out the best. Each one of us can relate to some of those stories in the Bible, and I have only mentioned a few. If we look at the mess that we have gone through in life we will see that God allowed it so that we could learn from it and try to live a better life. Often, when uninvited circumstances come into our lives, we cry out: "Why me Lord?" What we fail to see is that God knows us better than we know ourselves and when we go wrong, or perhaps do not follow the path that He has outlined for us, He allows some things to happen that will turn us around. We need to know that God still loves us and that He sometimes allows severe pain to come into our lives so that we may seek him and know the direction in which He wants us to proceed.

James 1:2–4 says: "Consider it pure joy, whenever you face trials of many kinds. Because you know that the testing of your faith develops perseverance. Perseverance must finish its work so that you may be mature and complete, not lacking anything." When a mess comes into our lives it is nothing but the trials that James speaks about here. The problem is that we fail to follow God's instructions, rather than finding joy in our difficult situations and the trials that we are going through. We tend to get very upset, allowing these circumstances to stress us out, resulting in the sense that our lives are out of control.

In my testimony about my life I can now see as far back as I can remember how trials, disappointments, hard times, abuse, failures, shortcomings, lack of resources, and abilities that I thought I needed and wanted but did not have, have helped me to persevere and pursue that which God had in store for me.

My life started off with the mess of being oversize at birth to the point that the midwife could not handle it and my dad had to get the doctor. Then, growing up as a sharecropper's son in the 1940s, 50s, and 60s stopped me from going to school on a regular basis and getting that foundation that was needed to be a good student. I believe now that God allowed it for a reason. Certainly, one reason is that I might tell my story of how God brought me through that difficult situation. The inability to obtain the kind of education that would have helped me to pursue the avenues that I wished and planned helped me to be what I am today.

The mess of starting school in the first grade for one half of a year, and then moving to another county and being placed in a primary grade below the first grade worked out well in the end. If I had continued on in the first grade at that time I would have completed high school one year earlier and this may have resulted in missed opportunities that I have had and perhaps I might have been in the wrong place at the wrong time. If I had continued and was not placed back in my early life I may have missed the opportunity to meet and marry my wife of fifty years.

Another mess was starting hard work at the early age of four and a half, carrying gallon buckets of water to my parents while planting tobacco. Now, I do not regret that. In life I have met many people who have not been trained and prepared for the life of growing up, realizing that they had to work. After getting out of the navy, I went to school for three years on Saturdays to become a journeyman iron worker and a certified welder. As an ironworker we usually worked in pairs. Once I was asked if I knew why most of the guys wanted to work with me—I said no I don't know and that I didn't realize that they did. I was told yes, they did, and it was because I did most of the work. I never noticed it because I was there to give an honest day's work for an honest day's pay. I also would rather work than go back and forth to the bathroom all day trying to hide. When I was working it made the day go by faster. Because of this mess God allowed me to see that if I was going to put forth this kind of effort for another company, that I could do it for myself by owning and running my own business. So there lies the beauty in that mess.

While working as an ironworker I found that it was often a dangerous job. I was an eyewitness to the deaths of six fellow ironworkers. There were a number of times when I barely escaped death myself. When I watched two men die when the crane cable broke and the bucket they were in fell ninety feet, I often asked: "Why not me?" After all, I had been in that bucket just twenty minutes before. This experience was a life changer for me: I saw life differently and was determined to be obedient to carry out the work that God had called me to do.

I would never say that God causes a mess, but I do believe that He allows messy things to happen so that He can get our attention and bring us back to where He wants us to be. I have found that a tough life makes us stronger, and that even sickness helps to bring us closer to God. My life has not been an easy one, but I can see many who are worse off. I am very proud to say that I always look at others being greater than myself. While that is partly the result of how some people in the world made me feel, I am also happy that God allowed this mess in my life to keep me humble. I can say that I was never jealous of any of my sisters and brothers or anyone else, but I always looked up to others and tried to allow their talents and abilities to motivate me to do more and to do better.

There was a mess in my family life while growing up. I was exposed to a lot of things that God did not approve of within our family. I believe that helped me to focus more strongly upon my marriage and the raising of our family.

The difficulties that I had in school—such as not being able to go to school a good portion of the time—kept my grades very low. I was told in the last year in school that I was not college material and that I should concentrate on being a good farmer. That statement turned out to be a motivator for me rather than a hindrance. It did not produce the feeling that I was a "nobody." Rather, I believe that God allowed this to happen to make me more humble and so that I would have a greater sensitivity towards others who may have experienced some of the same difficulties or circumstances that were even worse. I also believe that statement pushed me to prove that I did not have to remain a sharecropper/farmer.

A mess occurred at home the year that I graduated from high school. I wanted to go to college, but could not because of low grades and a lack of funds. As I continued to work on the farm that summer a real mess occurred within the family farming that caused me to join the armed forces. When I went to the recruiter's office and took the test to go into the Air

Force I later found out that it was a mess. The Air Force recruiter said that I was one point too low for the Air Force but that the Navy recruiter down the hall would probably take me. That was a mess because I found out that he had his quota for the month and he was now helping the Navy recruiter. I believe it turned out for the best because in the Navy there were fewer chances of going to the war in Vietnam. While I was being transported to the train station to go to boot camp another mess occurred. I was riding in the back of the recruiter's car and heard him discussing with another recruit who was in the front seat with him how he disliked black folks/African Americans. I had to hold my peace and I do praise God for allowing the Holy Spirit to work in me in that circumstance or I may not have made it to boot camp.

In boot camp I had a chance to become the leader of our group, but I lost that chance because I was not able to swim. I was asked to serve in that capacity because our commander saw that I had been co-captain of my high school football team. However, God works in mysterious ways and he took the fear out of me, and I learned to swim. I became a leader in other ways. In a godly way others looked up to me to be their spiritual leader during the entire time in boot camp. After boot camp my specialty and training should have resulted in my becoming an aircraft mechanic, but instead I was put into the position of barber—a hobby I had performed on the farm. When I look at these circumstances—which at the time was against my will—I find as life continues that God was intervening on my behalf to allow those unwanted situations to occur so that He could bring the best out of me for God's purpose and for me.

I attempted to write this autobiography a little over twenty years ago to speak mostly about the success that God had given me in the business world. In the midst of doing so a mess occurred that delayed and prohibited the completion of the writing at that time. I had paid a great deal of money to someone to assist me in the writing but they did not follow through, and all of the materials and recordings of interviews with people who knew me were misplaced and never surfaced again. Now that I am retired I feel that God allowed this mess as well because perhaps the focus was on the wrong things at that time. The focus and experience of God's deliverance is much greater now than it would have been twenty years ago.

There have been many situations in my life where a mess has occurred. Personally, I have made many mistakes in my youth, in my marriage, in the workplace, in my business life, in my church life, and in the ministry.

However, when I looked back over my life and the mistakes that caused the mess, I tried to capitalize on that. Rather than being discouraged and hanging my head and wanting to give up, I began to realize that God allowed those things to happen so that I could learn and grow and in all things come to Him and confess my sins and wrongdoing.

The mess of the sickness that occurred in my body in 2009 showed me that when these kind of things happen the devil seems to get even busier. The next mess occurred within the church where I pastored. The church is where you expect to go to get comfort, and when people see that you are down you expect that they would try and lift you up. Instead, confusion came within the church. This was not surprising for as we study God's Word it tells us that whenever you try to do what is right and be obedient, that Satan is very active. I did not fear Satan but the confusion slowed the progress of the church and combined with the other messy things that were going on, bringing some hurt. In the end, it affected the first lady more than the pastor.

The back pain that I had, being diabetic, and this church disturbance caused an increase in my blood pressure that at times went so high that the doctors could not believe that I was still alive. However, I know that God carried me through that mess so that I would recover and so that He could show me that the best is yet to come. An improvement in my health did not come easily or by lying around weeping and moaning. Rather, it came with hard work, a lot of discipline in eating, and a commitment to physical therapy, mostly on my own. I found that even in a mess you can live through it as long as you have a sincere desire to live and know who and what you are living for.

The messes did not stop coming just because we retired. Retirement brings on new challenges in life. Although we felt that we could relax and do less work, we also had to remember that retirement comes with some major financial changes, and times of quiet that can be upsetting when we focus on the past. We have had to deal with many financial challenges since retirement and discovered that all the things we tried to put into place before retirement do not always work out. When economic conditions follow a downward swing, just about all retirement financial conditions change as well. It has been a struggle but God has made a way. Many people cannot see or understand what we have had to go through financially, but again I say that God allows a mess to bring out the best. The best as I see it results when you put your total faith and trust in God so that He will make a way.

There are also times when we are quietly looking over our lives, considering how great retirement could be if we had just listened to God telling us to do things differently. For, as I look back over my life, I recognize many times when I should have done things differently and it would have made a great difference in my life now. Those thoughts can be very hurtful, but then when I think it over I also know that God allowed it in order to fulfill His overall purposes in my life.

We have had to travel the road a lot since retirement due to different circumstances that occurred in our lives and in the lives of our family. In most cases we travel with very little or no backup of cash. God has allowed us to travel without incidents and to return home safely. Again, I feel that God allowed this so we would put our total trust in him. This also brought us closer to God as we prayed more consistently—five, six, and sometimes twelve hours while driving on the dangerous highways. God is not through with us yet and I can see now that he has more for us to do. It seems as though He is saying: "you completed one phase of the ministry that I called you to do: now it is time to start the second phase."

I believe He allowed this mess in our lives to get our full attention, so that I could refocus on a ministry that I have outlined in a paper that I wrote while in seminary. The paper was entitled, "Helping the underprivileged to become Christian entrepreneurs." That was what I felt God was calling me to do when I ran businesses during the 1970s, 80s, and 90s.

I feel that if the economic climate is going to change in the African-American community and other communities that are poverty stricken then we have to focus on economic empowerment. We need to encourage and train young people about how to become economically empowered. I believe that we have been too selfish at times, wanting to get ahead in life ourselves but not encouraging and training our young people about the real economics of life. It is important to explain to them that they will be left behind unless they have a strong work ethic and a desire to improve their economic condition.

The mess that has occurred in my life has caused me to refocus and accept God's direction. For the balance of my life, as long as I am able, I will try and work with both young adults and older adults to help them to become dedicated Christian entrepreneurs.

I plan to do this through the new ministry organization that we have formed called "Ministry of Remembrance." The goal of this ministry is to reach back and help others. As outlined in Galatians 6:2–5: "Carry each other's burdens, and in this way you will fulfill the law of Christ. If anyone thinks they are something when they are not they deceive themselves. Each one should test their own actions. Then they can take pride in themselves alone, without comparing themselves to someone else, for each one should carry his own load." If God has blessed us with a talent and the ability to be successful, we should always be willing to reach back and help others to fulfill their God-given abilities as well. There are those who have greater abilities than I do and I plan to challenge them to help us to reach back and help others. I believe we all need to understand that none of us made it on our own. I strongly resonate with the song "If I Can Help Somebody" by Alma Bazel Androzzo and recorded so beautifully by Mahalia Jackson. I must help others in order for my life not to have been in vain. In this life we have to be trees that bear fruit, and if not we are no good to anyone, therefore our lives are wasted.

CHAPTER 12

Sharecropping for Christ

In this chapter I would like to introduce a new understanding of the word sharecropping. Sharecropping is both a concept and a reality that is truly embedded within me. I am sure that it is there because, as you have read in the previous chapters, this was all I knew as I grew up and what we as a family understood. My parents and all of our family before them were sharecroppers. Sharecropping seems to be a forgotten occupation and term. I have placed a reference to a history of sharecropping in the appendix. This description, provided by the Hampton Institute at Hampton University, explains the history of sharecropping and how it started after the Civil War.

In reading this book you have no doubt come to realize that I disliked sharecropping/farming for a variety of reasons. In an effort to introduce some hope to my memories and experience of sharecropping, I spoke with a retired theologian and professor of preaching. While we talked about what we had experienced in our early lives in connection with sharecropping, he threw out the statement "Sharecropping for Christ." As I thought about it, some very moving ideas and thoughts came into my spirit. Then I began to think about the similarity between sharecropping for owners of a farm, and sharecropping for Christ.

When the term sharecropping comes to mind, we think of farming and dealing directly with the soil. In the Bible we find a number of scripture references that deal with the soil of the earth. There is one scripture that stands out: "Then the Lord God formed man from the dust of the ground and breathed into his nostrils the breath of life, and the man became a living being." (Gen. 2:7) As I continued to search the scriptures with reference to sharecropping, I discovered an array of similarities between sharecropping on a farm, and the ministry of the gospel of Jesus Christ. First, I recognized seven basic characteristics of sharecropping:

1. Sharecropping resulted when the slaves were freed and the plantation owners had no one to work their fields (soil).

2. Sharecropping is hard work.

3. The work is never done.

4. Sharecroppers never own anything.

5. Sharecroppers are always in debt.

6. Sharecroppers move from place to place.

7. In sharecropping, the harvest is plenteous but the laborers are few.

The characteristics of sharecropping for Christ are basically the same, but they have a different purpose. First, just as the slaves were freed, Christ died on the cross and freed us from our sin. This means that we no longer have to be bound or tied up with Satan in sin, and we are free to serve God. However, Satan is always trying to get us to come back and do work for him and to tend what he calls his land.

Second, just as farming and sharecropping were hard work, so we find that working for Christ is hard work. It is essential to be totally dedicated to Him and to the work that He calls us to do. It is similar to working as a farmer, rising early and often working late into the night. The hard work consists of dealing with the four types of soil that Jesus describes in Matthew 13:3–9. We find that the soil is not always the same on the farm. When we sow the seeds and they fall on the different types of soil they have to be treated differently. The cultivation, the watering, and the total care are not the same. Jesus makes this comparison as he describes the four types of soil in the book of Matthew. There is hard work in sharecropping for Christ because we have the word of God falling on different kinds of people. For some, the cultivation of the heart and mind becomes difficult. In sharecropping for Christ we have to treat different souls with different care in order for them to grow and produce.

The third point in sharecropping for Christ is that the work is never done. Work is never done when you are sharecropping on a farm: there is always work to do in preparation for the next season. The work involves the planting of the seeds, weeding and cultivating the plants, irrigating, and caring for the growth of the seed and plant by fertilizing. After that, one must prepare the harvest for its final destination. When we are ministering for Christ we find it to be similar because the work for Christ is never done. As we work for Christ we have to always prepare for the next day, the next week, or the next season. We have to plant the word of God into people: training them and showing them the godly way of life so that they may mature and be fruitful. The work of the Christian and of those who are called to special ministry is never done.

The fourth point in sharecropping for Christ is that we never own anything. While sharecropping on the farm you never get to own a part of it for yourself. You simply work the land and produce the harvests, but the land is never yours. It is clear to those of us who are Christian that everything we have belongs to Christ. We sometimes get the feeling and take the attitude that we own something. We often say that we worked hard for what we have. Sometimes we say: "I'm not going to let anybody or anything take away what I have earned." Then one day God comes by and takes it all away and lets us know who owns what.

The fifth point in sharecropping for Christ is that you are always in debt. As we worked on the farm from year to year we were in debt all the time. When there was not a good harvest, we were not able to pay back the money borrowed during the year. Christ died on the cross for our sin. He died so that we could have life and have it more abundantly. We will always be indebted to our Lord and Savior for our freedom that we may obtain eternal life.

The sixth point in sharecropping for Christ is that there is a need to move from place to place. As sharecroppers we often moved from place to place. In most cases, the move was due to the growth within our family, and the need for better accommodation. In order to care for our family's needs, we had to move to different locations. In "The Great Commission" in Matthew 28:16–20 Jesus told His disciples to go to all nations, baptizing in the name of the Father and of the Son and of the Holy Spirit. As disciples of Christ, we are expected to go where He leads us to preach, teach, baptize, and make more disciples. We cannot put our tent pegs so deep into the ground that we cannot pull them up quickly and move to where God wants us to go.

The seventh point that is similar to sharecropping on the farm has to do with the harvests. Often, when a crop was ready for harvest, it came in so fast that there was a need for help. When this happened we hired outside help, or three or four families came together to work at harvesting the crops. Luke 10:2 states that the harvest is plenteous but the laborers are few. There is a need to train Christians to be leaders. There are many who want to know about Christ and have a desire to be converted, but we find it difficult to locate those who are willing to go and reach out to the lost souls so that they can be saved.

I found a new spiritual depth to my life as a sharecropper when I considered that I learned things that served me well when the time came for me to serve Jesus Christ. Jesus can truly bring His presence and His word to the darkest and most hopeless of places.

Appendix A[1]

Invoice to George Womack (1955)

F. S. Hayden was the man who owned the farm where the Womack family was employed. This 1955 invoice indicates the amount of money that the family had to live on a weekly basis. It also shows how the family was never able to get out of debt. As can be seen below, the balance due to Mr. Hayden from 1954 was $31.79. At the end of 1955 the family owed Mr. Hayden $82.49. With the exception of three years when a small profit was realized, the year 1954–1955 is a typical example of what happened during the fifteen years that the Womacks were sharecroppers on the Hayden farm.

F. S. HAYDEN
Electrical Contractor
ENGINEERING – CONSTRUCTION
1955   CREWE, VIRGINIA
Invoice to George Womack

Balance due from 54		31.79	Check No.
12–14-54	Advance	100.00	178
12–30	"	25.00	183
1–8	"	25.00	186
1–15	"	25.00	193
1–22	"	25.00	197
1–24	"	150.00	198

1. F. S. HAYDEN, Electrical Contractor, Crewe, Virginia, Invoice to George Womack, 1955. This table is an exact duplication of the original invoice.

1–29	"	25.00	200
2–4	"	25.00	205
2–12	"	25.00	208
2–19	"	25.00	211
2–21	"	15.00	213
2–26	"	25.00	214
3–5	"	25.00	217
3–12	"	25.00	220
3–16	"	50.00	225
3–26	"	25.00	231
3–31	"	25.00	232
4–9	"	25.00	234
4–13	Electric Motor	14.89	
4–16	Advance	25.00	239
4–16	"	10.00	242
4–23	"	25.00	245
4–30	"	25.00	247
5–7	"	25.00	254
5–14	"	25.00	259
5–14	"	225.00	260
5–21	"	25.00	263
5–28	"	25.00	265
5–28	Recap. 2 Tires	17.31	
6–5	Advance	25.00	274
6–11	"	25.00	276
6–18	"	25.00	278
6–29	25 straw 31 May	8.40	
6–25	Advance	25.00	280
7–2	"	25.00	286
7–9	"	25.00	293
7–16	"	25.00	296
7–22	"	25.00	299
7–30	"	25.00	301

8–6	"	25.00	304
8–13	"	25.00	306
8–20	"	25.00	311
8–26	"	25.00	313
9–3	"	25.00	317
9–10	"	25.00	319
9–17	"	25.00	322
9–24	"	25.00	325
10–1	Advance	25.00	326
10–8	"	25.00	329
10–15	"	25.00	331
10–22	"	25.00	334
10–30	"	25.00	337
11–2	"	25.00	339
11–5	"	25.00	340
11–12	"	25.00	344
11–19	"	25.00	349
11–26	"	25.00	353
12–3	"	25.00	360
110–35 Bales Hay		21.75	
5-Tel. call from Lawerence		2.25	
Fert. Oil, Supplies		442.47	
Total Owed		$2313.86	
	Payments		
1/29/55	Labor	20.00	
10/4	Tobacco	111.00	
10/11	"	227.83	
10/19	"	135.17	
10/25	"	186.80	

11/2	"	176.59	
11/4	"	243.88	
11/10	"	293.29	
11/17	"	551.97	
11/28	"	116.27	
11/29	"	13.61	
12/30	"	136.20	
12/6/	"	18.76	
Total paid		$2231.37	
Total Owed		$2313.86	
Total Paid		$2231.37	
		$ 82.49	Owed F.S.H.
December 6, 1955			Dec. 6, 1955

Appendix B
Sharecropping: A History That Appears Forgotten

Sharecropping began right after the U.S. Civil War. Former slave owners, many of whom could not pay wages to the whole complement of laborers necessary for productive harvests on their plantations, developed a farming arrangement that could compensate for the free labor—i.e., slaves—they no longer had available. In theory, under sharecropping, one-third of the crop proceeds would go to the landowner, another third to the laborer, and the final third to the individual or group that provided farming equipment, fertilizer, seeds, and so forth. However, in practice, landowners would frequently shortchange the black workers—depriving them of their just recompense. Sometimes, the tenant farmer would supply a portion of the seeds and other resources, and would expect due payment for them as well—oftentimes meeting with the same results, deficient remuneration. Across the South, former slaves were unable to make livable wages to take care of their families because of this form of pilfering.

There were many forms of sharecropping that developed. For example, landowners and freedmen would routinely contract with each other. On many occasions, the white owner would loan farming tools and resources to the black farmer as IOUs, and then collect after harvest—thus, reducing the final pay to the tenant. Landowners would tack on fees and other costs to further minimize compensation to the workers. Sometimes, the farmer would own his plot of land, but would still need to borrow equipment and seeds to cultivate it. After harvest, he would owe rental companies and other providers—significantly reducing his take-home pay and often suffering thievery in the final calculus. This type of injustice was quite pervasive in the South, and in many instances it perpetuated a de facto system of slavery far into the twentieth century in contradistinction to the Thirteenth Amendment, which de jure abolished it.

Also, access the following link for an excellent article by Devon Douglas-Bowers from the Hampton Institute at Hampton University on the history of sharecropping: "Debt Slavery: The Forgotten History of Sharecropping": http://www.hamptoninstitution.org/sharecropping.html#. VivEdSuX8fA.

Appendix C
The Schedule and Activities of the USS *Wasp* During John Womack's Tour of Duty[1]

The USS *Wasp* CVS-18

The early part of 1963 saw *Wasp* conducting anti-submarine warfare exercises off the Virginia Capes and steaming along the Caribbean coast of Costa Rica in support of the presidential visit. On March 21, President Kennedy arrived at San Jose for a conference with the presidents of six Central American nations. After taking part in Fleet exercises off Puerto Rico, the carrier returned to Boston on April 4. From May 11–18, *Wasp* took station off Bermuda as a backup recovery ship for Major Gordon Cooper's historic Mercury space capsule recovery. The landing occurred as

1. Wikipedia contributors, "USS Wasp (LHD-1)," *Wikipedia, The Free Encyclopedia,* https://en.wikipedia.org/w/index.php?title=USS_Wasp_(LHD-1)&oldid=685419187

planned in the mid-Pacific near Midway Atoll, and carrier *Kearsage* picked up Cooper and his Faith 7 spacecraft. *Wasp* then resumed anti-submarine warfare exercises along the Atlantic seaboard and in the Caribbean until she underwent overhaul in the fall of 1963 for FRAM (Fleet Rehabilitation and Modernization) overhaul in the Boston Naval Shipyard.

In March 1964, the carrier conducted sea trials out of Boston. During April, she operated out of Norfolk and Narragansett Bay. She returned to Boston on May 4 and remained there until May 14, when she got underway for refresher training in waters between Guantánamo Bay, Cuba, and Kingston, Jamaica, before returning to her home port on June 3, 1964.

On July 21, 1964, *Wasp* began a round-trip voyage to Norfolk and returned to Boston on August 7. She remained there through September 8 when she headed, via the Virginia Capes operating area, to Valencia, Spain. She then cruised the Mediterranean, visiting ports in Spain, France, and Italy, and returned home on December 18.

The carrier remained in port until February 8, 1964, and sailed for fleet exercises in the Caribbean. Operating along the eastern seaboard, she recovered the Gemini IV astronauts and their spacecraft on June 7 after splashdown. Gemini IV was the mission of the first American to walk in space, Edward White. During the summer, the ship conducted search and rescue operations for an Air Force C-121 plane that had gone down off Nantucket. Following an orientation cruise for twelve congressmen on August 20–21, *Wasp* participated in joint training exercises with German and French forces. From December 16–18, the carrier recovered the astronauts of Gemini VI and VII after their splashdowns, and then returned to Boston on December 22 to finish out the year.

On January 24, 1966, *Wasp* departed Boston for fleet exercises off Puerto Rico. En route, heavy seas and high winds caused structural damage to the carrier. She put into Roosevelt Roads, Puerto Rico, on February 1 to determine the extent of her damage and affect as much repair as possible. Engineers were flown from Boston and decided that the ship could cease "Springboard" operations early and return to Boston. The ship conducted limited anti-submarine operations from February 6–8 prior to leaving the area. She arrived at Boston on February 18 and was placed in restricted availability until March 7 when her repair work was completed.

Wasp joined in exercises in the Narragansett Bay operating areas. While the carrier was carrying out this duty, a television film crew from the National Broadcasting Company was flown to *Wasp* on March 21 and stayed on the ship during the remainder of her period at sea, filming material for a special color television show to be presented on Armed Forces Day.

The carrier returned to Boston on March 24, 1966 and was moored there until April 11. On March 27, Doctor Ernst Lemberger, the Austrian Ambassador to the United States, visited the ship. On April 18, the ship embarked several guests of the secretary of the navy and set courses for Guantánamo Bay. She returned to Boston on May 6. A week later, the veteran flattop sailed to take part in the recovery of the Gemini IX spacecraft. Embarked in *Wasp* were some sixty-six persons from NASA, the television industry, media personnel, an underwater demolition recovery team, and a defense department medical team. On June 6, she recovered astronauts Lieutenant Colonel Thomas P. Stafford and Lieutenant Commander Eugene Cernan and flew them to Cape Kennedy. *Wasp* returned their capsule to Boston.

Wasp participated in "ASWEX III," an anti-submarine exercise that lasted from June 20 through July 1, 1966. She spent the next twenty-five days in port at Boston for more upkeep. On July 25 the carrier got underway for "ASWEX IV." During this exercise, the Soviet intelligence collection vessel, *Agi Traverz*, entered the operation area necessitating a suspension of the operation and eventual repositioning of forces. The exercise was terminated on August 5. She then conducted a dependents' day cruise on August 8 and 9, and orientation cruises on the August 10, 11, and 22. After a two-day visit to New York, *Wasp* arrived in Boston on September 1 and underwent upkeep until September 19. From that day to October 4, she conducted hunter/killer operations with the Royal Canadian Navy aircraft embarked.

Following upkeep at Boston, the ship participated in the Gemini XII recovery operation from November 5–18, 1966. The recovery took place on November 15 when the space capsule splashdown occurred within three miles (five km) of *Wasp*. Captain James A. Lovell and Major Edwin E. Aldrin were lifted by helicopter hoist to the deck of *Wasp* and there enjoyed two days of celebration. *Wasp* arrived at Boston on November 18 with the Gemini XII spacecraft on board. After off-loading the special Gemini support equipment, *Wasp* spent ten days making ready for her next period at sea.

On November 28 *Wasp* departed Boston to take part in the Atlantic Fleet's largest exercise of the year, "Lantflex-66," in which more than one hundred United States ships took part. The carrier returned to Boston on December 16 where she remained through the end of 1966.

Wasp served as carrier qualification duty ship for the Naval Air Training Command from January 24 to February 26, 1967 and conducted operations in the Gulf of Mexico and off the east coast of Florida. She called at New Orleans for Mardi Gras on February 4–8, at Pensacola on February 11–12, and at Mayport, Florida, on February 19–20. Returning to Boston a week later, she remained in port until March 19 when she sailed for "Springboard" operations in the Caribbean. On March 24, Wasp joined Salamonie for an underway replenishment but suffered damage during a collision with the oiler. After making repairs at Roosevelt Roads, she returned to operations on March 29 and visited Charlotte Amalie, St. Thomas, United States Virgin Islands, and participated in the celebration from March 30 to April 2, which marked the fiftieth anniversary of the purchase of the Virgin Islands from Denmark by the United States. Wasp returned to Boston on April 7, remained in port for four days, and then sailed to Earle, New Jersey to off-load ammunition prior to overhaul. She visited New York for three days before returning to the Boston Naval Shipyard, where she began an overhaul on April 21, 1967, which was not completed until early 1968.

Gemini IX astronauts Cernan and Stafford aboard Wasp on June 9, 1966

Appendix D
Selected Newspaper Articles

"FROM BUCKET AND MOP TO $2M IN SALES"[1]

By Roger Morency
Business Editor

PEABODY—In 1977 John Womack—ex-firefighter, ex-steelworker, Navy veteran—began John's Janitorial Service Inc. out of his Salem home with a bucket and a mop.

Thursday he was honored at Satch's restaurant in Boston as New England Minority Businessman of the Year by the Minority Businessman Development Agency of the Department of Commerce.

Additionally, today he attended a ceremony at the Bank of Boston where he was acknowledged as second runnerup to the New England Small Businessman of the Year selected by the U. S. Small Business Administration.

Along the way his janitorial service has grown from that bucket and mop to a full maintenance and servicing firm with 200 full-and part-time employees, operating in four of the New England states, generating a projected $2 million in sales for 1983.

Womack, who is deacon of his church, explains his motivation and success in terms of his "ministry."

1. Morency, "From bucket and mop to $2m in sales."

"I would like to show young people that you don't have to have a lot of degrees to succeed and there is something for them in this world if they are willing to work hard," Womack said. Even so, he has found the time to further his own business education in night school and through other programs.

The 39-year-old Womack, a huge and soft-spoken man, concedes to a nodding acquaintance with adversity. Prior to starting his janitorial service, and after leaving the Navy, the transplanted Virginian worked seven years as a steelworker, and a couple of years as a firefighter while holding down a supervisory job with one of the larger industrial cleaners in the area. It was a lot of hours and a lot of hard work.

His entrepreneurial venture just sort of happened. After a few weeks with the bucket and mop, he borrowed $900 and bought his first cleaning machine. He paid that off in two weeks and bought another machine,

In 1979 he borrowed $10,000 from the SBA and bought more equipment and a truck. The business grew, and in August of 1980 he resigned from the Salem Fire Department and gave the business his undivided attention. At the time he had 60 employees and annual sales were at the $380,000 mark.

"It was a matter of choosing the opportunity against the security of the fire department job," Womack explained.

In November of that year Womack bought the land and building at 197 Washington St., which is the headquarters of the firm now.

Like any successful business that wants to stay competitive and continue to grow, John's Janitorial Service is now in the hands of a board of directors and is diversifying. The seven-member board is made up of some of the area's more successful blacks from the professions and industry.

"It's a good board, and eight heads are better than one," pointed out Womack. The firm has also branched into shelf stocking with the commissary store at Pease Air Force Base, one of the bigger customers in this category. There are also plans on the drawing board for an addition at 197 Washington St. which will be a wholesale and retail outlet for cleaning supplies.

John's Janitorial has also won a contract to clean the cars of one of the MBTA lines, and is in the process of bidding on others.

The firm has been awarded contracts with some of the area's major industrial, commercial and service firms. There are contracts with the U.

S. Army for the post exchange at Fort Devens, the Barnes Defense Support Activity Building (the old Fargo building in Boston), the University of Massachusetts at Boston, Parker Brothers, Ventron, New England Telephone and 40 or 50 other clients.

"We are anticipating significant growth to continue for the next three to five years," Womack explained. He has also lined up a line of credit with one area bank, after another, with which he had been doing business, told him the company was growing too fast.

Womack shrugged at the thought and said, "We are growing fast, but we are growing carefully."

Given the results since 1977, who can dispute it?

RAGS TO RICHES STORY:
FORMER SHARECROPPER OWNS BUSINESS[2]

M. Brenda Smith

In the 1950s John Womack was a sharecropper in South Hills, Va. Today he is the owner of John's Janitorial Service in Peabody, Mass., and the proud recipient of this year's New England Minority Businessman of the Year award from the Minority Business Development Agency of the Department of Commerce.

In addition, he was recently acknowledged as the second runner-up for the New England Small Businessman of the Year award given by the U.S. Small Business Administration.

Womack came to Boston in the early 1960s with the Navy. After serving four years on the aircraft carrier, U.S.S. Wasp, he went to work for a record company in Woburn.

"I decided there was no future in that job," said Womack, "so I left." From 1970 to 1976, he was an iron worker but decided he needed a job where he wasn't subjected to so many layoffs. So, he became a fireman in Salem, Mass.

"All the time I was working there," he said, "I was also working part-time as a supervisor in a cleaning company. I've always had two or three jobs at a time." When the cleaning company lost the janitorial contract in the building Womack supervised, he decided to go out on his own.

2. Smith, "Rags to Riches Story: former sharecropper owns business."

He started with a bucket, a mop and one buffer. He ran his new business out of his home in Salem. "I started with small jobs," he said. "After a few weeks I borrowed $900 from an uncle for a rug machine. I sent his money back in two weeks and bought another rug machine. Business has been good ever since."

While still working as a firefighter, Womack continued to run his cleaning business out of his house. "I kept pursuing it and adding accounts," he said. By 1980, he had seven or eight accounts and 60 employees. It was time to make a decision—keep both jobs or quit one.

By November 1980, he resigned from the Salem Fire Department and moved his business into offices in Peabody. "I hired my first secretary," he said, "and got my first contract through the Small Business Administration."

By early 1981, Womack's business volume topped $380,000 and he had hired 40 more people. Today he employs 200 people (full and part-time) and projects that he will top $2 million in sales this year.

John's Janitorial Service has contracts with the Federal Government as well as with private companies. He also cleans private homes.

Womack wants to begin marketing a special service, shelf stocking, to both the public and private sector. His company now stocks shelves in the commissary.

WOMACK'S FIRM WAS BUILT FROM THE GROUND UP[3]

By Ray Routhier

PEABODY—When John Womack's janitorial business became successful, he bought himself a Mercedes-Benz. After all, he labored and sacrificed to build the business. He wanted his family to have some of the "good" things in life. Womack, however, found that he was uncomfortable with the car.

"When people would see me drive up in the car, they'd treat me different because they thought I was rich," said the softspoken Womack. "I resented that. That's not what I'm about."

He soon traded in the Mercedes for a Plymouth Voyager.

Womack built his business, John's Janitorial Service, Inc., with faith and a determination to be his own boss. He began seven years ago as the

3. Routhier, "Womack's firm was built from the ground up."

sole employee of the company, armed with a bucket and a mop. Womack now employs 275 people and annual sales are over $2 million.

Womack said he is proud of his company's growth, but more than that, he is proud to control his own destiny.

"I wanted to provide for my family. I worked hard at all the other jobs I had, but someone else was in control," he said. "I wanted to be in control of my family's future."

Womack was one of ten children in a family of Virginia sharecroppers. The family was very poor, and Womack attended school only about half the time, working on the land the rest of the time. He grew up in a strongly religious environment, and he credits all his success to the blessings of God.

"All the people who've helped me didn't have to help me," said Womack firmly. "God is surrounding me with people and things, and I just had to use my common sense and work hard at getting the most from them. Some people call things that happen to them luck. Well, I don't believe in luck, I believe in God."

A Navy veteran, Womack worked as a salesman, an iron worker and a firefighter before starting his own business. In addition to his full-time jobs, Womack held several part-time positions, including that of supervisor for a large janitorial firm in Boston.

Alone, with his bucket and mop, Womack started his business by running up and down Route 1 cleaning motel rooms for $5 and $7 a unit. He quickly learned that an unproven janitorial business doesn't bring in a lot of customers. He did a lot of carpet cleaning and house cleaning, just trying to get by.

Womack bought his first cleaning machine with $900 he borrowed from his blind uncle Daniel, who worked a dishwashing machine in Roanoke, Va.

His small jobs eventually led to bigger cleaning jobs, and he didn't let a few rejections slow him down.

"I got a little impatient when people kept telling me that I couldn't do what I knew I could do," he said. "When you have no track record, you just have to keep trying until someone will believe in you."

His first big job was cleaning the cafeterias at Salem State College, and then he got a contract for the Peabody Office Building. The business expanded to 60 employees in 1980, and that's when Womack resigned from the Salem Fire Department and moved the business from his home in Salem to its present location at 197 Washington Street.

Womack's client list now includes: Fort Devens Army Base, Pease Air Force Base, Eastman Gelatine Company, Massachusetts Bay Transportation Authority (MBTA), the State Transportation Building and UMass Boston.

Womack says that his business has flourished partly because he decided early to "run a business like a business." He incorporated while still working out of his home and formed a board of directors. The board included people who Womack considers honest and "would speak their mind." Womack said he listened and learned from these people.

Last December Womack opened Peabody Paper and Industrial Supply Co. at his Washington Street address. The new enterprise is part of Womack's overall plan to diversify and grow, getting as many people involved as possible. He is proud that his one-man operation has grown to provide jobs for so many people.

Womack said he would like his business to be an example for young people to follow. He was strongly influenced as a boy by his 4-H leader, and he wants to help young people himself. Womack has worked with youths through his church, the Black Forum, the Big Brother Association and was asked to sit on the Board of Directors of the YMCA. He said he likes talking with kids one on one, and showing them that hard work can bring success, as in his case.

"I want kids to see, especially kids who can't go to college, that they can be as good as any other human being," said Womack from behind his sprawling desk. "I like to hire young people so they can see how a business operates, so they can be involved and so they'll see what hard work gets you."

Womack attained his success through intense desire and determination. He knows he worked hard for what he has, but he says it took more than hard work. His faith in God is what carried him to where he is today.

"Growing up, we had to have faith to carry us from day to day. The trials and tribulations I had starting my business seem minor to those I knew as a child," he said.

"After being that poor and seeing so much hardship, nothing could stop me."

SUCCESS STORY[4]

John Womack's story is one that can —and should—help keep the American dream alive.

As was noted in Friday's news, Womack began a janitorial service out of his Salem home in 1977. Starting with a mop and bucket, the basic tools of the trade, the Salem firefighter was looking to build his own business. And he certainly succeeded—to the point where, in 1980, he resigned from the fire department to devote full time to the fledgling business, which had already grown to 60 employees and annual sales in the range of $380,000.

The success story continues. Last week, Womack was honored as New England Minority Businessman of the Year and was also runnerup in the New England Small Businessman of the Year competition.

John's Janitorial Service, operating out of offices in Peabody, now has 200 employees, does work in four New England states, and should generate revenues of $2 million this year. Womack, 39, counts numerous industrial, commercial and service firms among his clientele, and also has a number of government service contracts.

Womack's view of his company's success is one keyed on hard work and good service. These are good cornerstones for anyone's ambitions.

4. "Success Story."

Appendix E
A Ministry of Mission: Mobilizing the Underprivileged to Become Christian Entrepreneurs

As I struggle with my call to the ministry, I feel that God is telling me not to try and be someone I'm not. Rather, I feel called to lead, teach, and motivate others on how God brought me out of the poverty of share-cropping in Virginia to where I am today. I keep hearing the cry from black men to be role models for those who are still in poverty. It seems that the spirit of God persists in telling me not only that we need role models, but also that I must bear witness to what God has done for me and through me.

I am being drawn to a ministry that seems to be different from any other ministry I have seen. God has worked miracles in my life and in the lives of my family. According to the standards of the dominant culture, we were undereducated, underprivileged, and impoverished until graduation from high school. In spite of that deprivation, God has blessed me to have much more than I thought possible. I know that I did not obtain what I have on my own; consequently, I am being led by the spirit to let people know how God has worked in my life so that I can tell, show, teach, and lead others to become solid Christian entrepreneurs. Most of the time, I still see myself as unqualified to do what God wants me to do. However, the Lord is persistent and his blessings have resulted in a reverence for God that is greater than the joy I could have from anything else I can do.

In my calling to the ministry, I long to be on the staff of a church to work under its pastor: one who would give me special duties and responsibilities. I would like to start an outreach ministry—a mission to help to mobilize underprivileged people to become Christian entrepreneurs. Also, this ministry would reach out to those people—mostly youth, but older folks as well—who feel that they do not have a place in society, because of their lack of education. Many think they do not have the ability to attain the knowhow to start a business because of low grades in school and lack of finances.

In order to alleviate this misperception, I would like to have a number of fellowship breakfasts in a designated community location. During these gatherings, I would work to assist those who want to go into business as well as those who have just started a business. I would like to accomplish this endeavor with the support of other local leaders. The purpose of these mealtime meetings would be to get the business community to buy into this enterprise and to convince them to become involved. I would seek the help of other entrepreneurs in establishing forums and seminars to help train people to begin to identify and prosecute the abilities God has given them. This training would be grounded in the fact that God has a plan for everybody, and the vital importance of having faith and believing in themselves and, more importantly, in God.

To accomplish these goals, the leaders of this multifaceted effort need to know how to attract residents of the specified area: to meet the people where they are, and find out what they feel their needs are and what the obstacles are to achieving their objectives. Part and parcel of such foundational development is counseling the people on dealing with others, strengthening their self-esteem, and transcending difficult situations. As the participants become clear about their mission, purpose, and vision, they would orally present to their classmates and even to fellow local residents about how hard it was to redirect themselves, and the importance of having mentors.

As I have hired and worked alongside multigenerational people in the cleaning and food industry, I have discovered that many, if not most, youth and young adults do not take themselves seriously and dupe themselves into thinking that there is nothing for them to do. Moreover, because they have not gone to college or acquired a marketable skill, they relinquish belief in the possibility that they still have a lot of potential and, unwarrantedly, in my opinion, simply abandon the pursuit of a better life. They need to understand that God did not make us carbon copies of each other: our idiosyncrasies and our foibles distinguish us as individuals, and God has something for each and every one of us to do. In imagining our bodies as having many different parts, we must realize that these parts have different functions, and that all parts of the body are important in order for the body to remain healthy. We are all different, but each one of us is important to keep God's body of people functioning, to keep the world healthy. No one should feel less or more important than anyone else.

This viewpoint of neighborliness sharpened for me when I read the thirteenth chapter of *Urban Church Education* by Donald B. Rogers, which discusses biblical storytelling.[1] Consequently, I have told my life story about how God helped and blessed me through the basic lens of biblical stories. For instance, I believe my story is closely related to the scriptural story of Joseph. I believe that Joseph's and my stories can serve as touchstones for others to relate to their own lives and the variety of possibilities and opportunities before them. By demonstrating how God took care of us in the midst of challenging and sometimes insidious occurrences, I believe increasing numbers of participants would try to start a business, acquire a better job, and/or appear in the church sanctuary for the first time in a while (if at all) and worship with fellow believers. Likewise, I think it is important for participants to tell stories about themselves, to discover ways their lives relate to characters in the Bible, and, in turn, to inspire others.

These entrepreneurial seminars would take place two to four times a year in different churches in the urban community. Students would research various kinds of subjects and objectives related to becoming expressly Christian businesspersons. Some of the central lessons in this process appear below:

1. The basic fundamentals of starting a business from scratch

2. How to determine what business best suits you

3. Positives and negatives of starting a business

4. Business ethics

5. How to get help and who can help

6. Setting up mentors for each new businessperson

1. Rogers, *Urban Church Education*.

I hope and pray that I will be able to get support and help from other pastors in the urban community to embark on this new kind of ministry. However, I feel this is what God is calling me to do. Consequently, regardless of the extent of collaboration with local religious leaders, I will press on towards my goals. I am prepared for whatever issues may come, because I am committed to this venture for the long haul. Although these attempts will not save the whole world, I am convinced blessings will abound once the program commences. If certified students could become prosperous or otherwise successful, they would undoubtedly serve as role models for aspiring youth. Partnerships with others are desirable, but the mission supersedes such alliances.

I believe that we have to do something outside the church building to get churchgoers' attention and to channel God's love. We may talk about love at church, but, oftentimes, the moment we step outside the edifice, we demur in helping the poor. A major issue is our unfamiliarity with the poor and our unwillingness to take the time to ensure that all have the basic necessities of life.

My intention for this ministry is to show the impoverished how to fish for themselves, so to speak. Young people in urban areas often feel isolated and unconsidered when they do not have the wherewithal to achieve what they need. In suburbia, it seems the young are given so much on a silver platter, yet remain unskilled in applying their knowledge constructively and productively. Frequently, they return home and seek assistance from their parents because they lack marketable skills—preventing them from learning how to fish, or fend, for themselves.

The ministry's work will be holistic in nature. The workshops, seminars, and discussions will help them define a strategy and distinguish among the necessities of life versus wants and desires. I hope that this will help the participants put things in the right perspective: trusting in a caring and compassionate God—not for self-aggrandizement, but, rather, for the alleviation of abject poverty. The ministry of mission to the underprivileged will help to mobilize participants to focus on their lives and strive to become Christian entrepreneurs.

In summary, I would like to start on a small scale by organizing breakfast meetings and planning sessions approximately once per month or every other month with a small group of people. Subsequently, perhaps in a year or two or three, I hope to ratchet them up to recur more often with increasingly larger audiences.

It is my prayer and hope that this ministry will help people no longer feel that they have any less ability than they perceive others to have. Rather, they will come to know more fully that God loves and cares for us all—regardless of our historical, traditional, or contemporary circumstances. After all, we are all somebody, for each and every one of us is a child of God!

Appendix F
Lord, Why Did You Make Me Black?

A Poem by RuNett Nia Ebo

Lord, Lord,
Why did You make me Black?
Why did You make me someone
The world wants to hold back?

Black is the color of dirty clothes;
The color of grimy hands and feet.
Black is the color of darkness;
The color of tire-beaten streets.

Why did you give me thick lips,
A broad nose and kinky hair?
Why did You make me someone
Who receives the hatred stare?

Black is the color of a bruised eye
When somebody gets hurt.
Black is the color of darkness.
Black is the color of dirt.

How come my bone structure's so thick;
my hips and cheeks are high?
How come my eyes are brown
and not the color of the daylight sky?

Why do people think I'm useless?
How come I feel so used?
Why do some people see my skin and think I should be abused?

Lord, I just don't understand;
What is it about my skin?
Why do some people want to hate me
And not know the person within?

Black is what people are "listed,"
When others want to keep them away.
Black is the color of shadows cast.
Black is the end of the day.

Lord, You know, my own people mistreat me;
And I know this just isn't right.
They don't like my hair or the way I look
They say I'm too dark or too light.

Lord, Don't You think it's time
For You to make a change?
Why don't You re-do creation
And make everyone the same?

(God answered)

Why did I make you black?
Why did I make you black?

Get off your knees and look around.
Tell Me, what do you see?
I didn't make you in the image of darkness.
I made you in the Likeness of ME!

I made you the color of coal
From which beautiful diamonds are formed.
I made you the color of oil,
The black-gold that keeps people warm.

I made you from the rich, dark earth
That can grow the food you need.
Your color's the same as the panther's
Known for (her) beauty and speed.

Lord, Why Did You Make Me Black?

Your color's the same as the Black stallion,
A majestic animal is he.
I didn't make you in the Image of darkness
I made you in the Likeness of Me!

All the colors of a Heavenly Rainbow
Can be found throughout every nation;
And when all those colors were blended well,
YOU ARE MY GREATEST CREATION.

Your hair is the texture of lamb's wool
Such a humble, little creature is he.
I am the Shepherd who watches them.
I am the One who will watch over thee.

You are the color of midnight-sky,
I put the stars' glitter in your eyes.
There's a smile hidden behind your pain
That's the reason your cheeks are high.

You are the color of dark clouds formed
When I send My strongest weather.
I made your lips full so when you kiss'
the one you love they will remember.

Your stature is strong; your bone structure, thick
to withstand the burdens of time.
The reflection you see in the mirror. . .
The Image looking back at you is MINE!

Bibliography

Bowers, Devon D. "Debt Slavery: The Forgotten History of Sharecropping." http://www.hamptoninstitution.org/sharecropping.html#.VivEdSuX8fA.

Hayden, F. S. Electrical Contractor, Crewe, Virginia, Invoice to George Womack (1955).

Jones, Rev. Kirk B. *Rest in the Storm: Self-Care Strategies for Clergy and Other Caregivers.* Valley Forge, PA: Judson, 2001.

Morency, Roger. "From Bucket and Mop to $2m in Sales." *Bay State Banner* (1983).

Rogers, Donald B. *Urban Church Education.* Birmingham, AL: Religious Education, 1989.

Routhier, Ray. "Womack's Firm Was Built from the Ground Up." *Peabody Times* (n.d.).

Smith, M. B. "Rags to Riches Story: Former Sharecropper Owns Business." *Peabody Times* (1987).

"Success Story." *Peabody Times* (1986).

Wikipedia contributors, "USS Wasp (LHD-1)," *Wikipedia, The Free Encyclopedia,* https://en.wikipedia.org/w/index.php?title=USS_Wasp_(LHD-1)&oldid=685419187.

Wolf, Richard. "Equality Still Elusive 50 Years After Civil Rights Act." *USA Today* (April 1, 2014). http://www.usatoday.com/story/news/nation/2014/01/19/civil-rights-act-progress/4641967/.

Note: The *Peabody Times* was a daily newspaper in operation from March 1924 through August 1995 in Peabody, Massachusetts.

www.ingramcontent.com/pod-product-compliance
Lightning Source LLC
Chambersburg PA
CBHW082105140626
46553CB00018B/685